OutdoorLife

THE ULTIMATE
WINTER
SURVIVAL
HANDBOOK

TIM MACWELCH
and the editors of *Outdoor Life*

weldon**owen**

CONTENTS

BASICS

CONTENTS

CONTENTS

WILDERNESS

WINTER IS THE GREAT EQUALIZER.

It freezes the rich and the poor, the sick and the healthy, the young and the old alike. But for those who are wise enough to prepare, or clever enough to adapt, winter's teeth don't bite so deeply. You'll know these people when you see them: They'll zip by on skis, or wave from their ice-fishing holes. They did their research, and they are making the most of our coldest season.

This book is your ticket to join these resiliant ranks—to live easier during the winter months, face the challenges of the cold, safely handle emergencies, and even survive a wintry catastrophe. There's no time like the present to prepare for winter's wrath.

Tim MacWelch

BASICS

THE SEASON OF ICE AND SNOW CAN BE HARD

on our bodies, homes, vehicles, and pets, but it's not without its rewards. At what other time of year could you make an ice rink in your backyard, catch a fish under the lake, or enjoy a little cross-country skiing to your neighbor's house? Only winter can provide these activities, though it requires caution above all else. The cold can be dangerous, and we need to ready ourselves for the extreme end of the temperature spectrum. Follow the squirrel's example and stock away food and supplies, learn how to prepare your home and vehicles for the cold months ahead, figure out what to wear, and find out how you can have a little fun in the coming deep freeze.

1 SHUT DOWN A HOME FOR WINTER

To avoid returning to a damaged dwelling, broken pipes, and ruined belongings, there are some important steps to take—both in and around the house—before a cold-weather exodus. Whether you're evacuating your house in an emergency or getting your summer home ready to stand empty all winter, you'll want to turn off the electricity. In a crisis, you may not have time to complete all of the winter prep shown here—so just be sure to take care of the water and power, and handle the rest as time allows.

FRIDGE Unplug the fridge, and empty all of the contents. Bring them with you, and prop the fridge and freezer doors open to prevent mold.

CABINETS OR PANTRY Bring any canned and jarred foods with you, as these containers will burst when frozen. Dry goods may be left behind, as they are not usually harmed by the cold; place them in metal containers to prevent rodents from having a party while you're gone.

WATER PIPE Turn off the water at the outside meter if you're on municipal water, or turn off your pump and empty the pressure tank if you're in a rural area with a well. Once turned off, open every faucet and valve in the home to drain all of the lines.

WATER HEATER Drain the water heater. Make sure you turn off the power first, if it's an electric unit, otherwise you'll burn up the heating elements.

TOILET TANK Once the water is off, flush the toilet to empty the tank. Any remaining water in the tank can be sopped up with a towel or mixed with a splash of antifreeze to prevent freeze damage.

TOILET BOWL After turning off the water and draining the lines and toilet tank, pour 1 liter (or quart) of rubbing alcohol or vehicle engine antifreeze into the bowl. This will prevent the water from freezing—which can break the toilet in half.

SINKS AND SHOWERS All sinks and showers will need the same antifreeze treatment as the toilet. Pour half a liter (or quart) of antifreeze in each drain right before leaving after you have used the fixture for the last time.

GAS METER Turn off any propane or LP gas that supplies the home. Make sure a professional turns the gas back on and checks all gas systems before you occupy the home again.

RAT TRAP Place mouse or rat traps around the home to catch any marauding mammals. Set them in places where the liquefying rodent won't damage the flooring.

DOORS AND WINDOWS Secure the doors and windows. Lock up tight with additional latches or locks at back doors and strips of wood in the tracks of any sliders. Ask a trustworthy friend to check on the place during your absence.

2 PREPARE YOUR PANTRY

Before the cold digs its claws in deep and you can see the back of your pantry, take some time to plan for your needs. Clean out your cupboards to take inventory of what you have (and ditch the expired stuff). Make a list of what you'll need on hand for emergencies like getting snowed in or a power outage. Buy the things that you know you'll need first, and any leftover funds can go toward the rest.

CANNED GOODS Choose high-calorie foods, favoring those that can be eaten straight from the can. Meaty stews, hearty soups, chili, and pasta dishes are all excellent choices.

DRY GOODS Dry goods will last a long time and won't freeze or burst like canned foods. Dry pasta is the highest-calorie dry staple, and you only need boiling water to prepare it. Rice, beans, oats, powdered milk, flour, cornmeal, and hard candy are also great selections.

FATS Olive oil, lard, ghee, coconut oil, and vegetable shortening can last a long time in cold conditions. They also provide the massive number of calories you'll need to work and play in frigid temperatures. Add a little fat to all of your meals for the calorie content and flavor.

DRINKS Hot cocoa, tea, coffee, and other hot beverages are important sources of warmth, calories, hydration, and morale. Stock an ample supply of family favorites.

3 REFRESH ESSENTIAL SUPPLIES

Before the first big storm of the season closes down the roads, make sure you've restocked these vital items.

WATER Don't forget a few gallons of water per person in case your water supply freezes.

LIGHTING You'll need fresh batteries for your flashlights—and a few backup candles.

FIRST-AID SUPPLIES Cuts and burns are common injuries. Keep burn cream and trauma dressings, adhesive bandages, and other supplies handy.

TP AND HYGIENE ITEMS Make sure you have abundant supplies of necessary bathroom products, disinfecting spray, and an emergency bucket "toilet" with a tight-fitting lid.

MORALE BOOSTERS Chocolate, cookies, and other treats are good sources of fat—and lifted spirits. A bottle of wine or other alcohol can be great (in moderate amounts) for the adults. Activity books and crayons are sanity-savers for parents, and a new board game is fun for the entire family. Hide these items well, and bring them out when the time is right.

4 WINTERIZE YOUR BOB

A BOB (Bug-Out Bag) is a collection of supplies for evacuation during a hazardous event. Typically it includes spare clothes, food, shelter gear, tools, first-aid kits, and communication and self-defense items. You should equip your gear with some winter-specific survival items, too.

Your clothes are your first line of defense against winter's grip. The last thing you want is a pile of shorts and T-shirts in the middle of February. Instead, stock your bag with wool- or synthetic-fiber clothing that can be layered for different temperatures and conditions. Gloves will save your hands from the constant wear and tear of survival tasks, and warm headgear will prevent heat loss.

Put a zero-degree or sub-zero sleeping bag in your BOB. Yes, these sleeping bags are big, heavy, and expensive. But there are few things that will help you more during a winter emergency than a bag built for the cold. A space blanket just isn't going to cut it in the dead of winter.

Buy a few 16-ounce (0.5-L) water bottles from the store, already filled. These are thin-walled and can handle the expansion caused by freezing. You can still keep larger bottles, but leave them empty during storage. Add some disinfection tablets to your gear, since your water filter could freeze up.

5 GET READY TO WINTERIZE

There is always work to be done before the colder weather sets in. We can see it in the hustle and bustle of the animal kingdom as the air cools—they know that winter is coming, and so do we. Follow this autumnal checklist of things to do (or to check) for the proper winterization of your home. Start with a visual inspection of your property and home's exterior, and finish off with the systems inside your home.

OUTSIDE

Check your roof for missing shingles, damaged flashing, popped-up nails, and other possible leak points.

Clean the fall foliage from your gutters while you're up there.

Place a cover over the condenser for your air-conditioning system; if you have window units, remove and store them for winter.

Turn off outside water spigots and drain them down or use an insulating cover.

Disconnect, drain, and store any garden hoses.

Put away any lawn items that would be harmed by freezing (such as bird baths).

INSIDE

Fire up your heating system for a test run (you may want a professional to do a tune-up), and replace all of the air filters.

If you use heating oil or propane, order an ample supply. If you rely on wood heat, cut or buy more firewood than you expect to use. Tie down tarps to keep your woodpiles dry.

Install a carbon monoxide detector and replace all smoke alarm batteries.

If you have a fireplace or woodstove, clean the chimney or stovepipe of soot, bird nests, and any other fire hazards. Have it professionally cleaned and inspected once every few years.

Inspect the chimney's flue damper. Make certain that it opens, closes, and locks into position.

Check the gauge on your fire extinguisher to make sure it's fully pressurized. If you don't have an extinguisher, get one!

6 STOP DRAFTS

The drafts around your home are caused by gaps, cracks, and openings, and they can waste a lot of your expensive winter heat. Stop the cold air from coming inside by knowing where drafts happen and how to fix them.

DOORS Doorways are a common site for drafts, and are fairly easy to repair. Check the rubbery weather stripping on the sides, bottom, and top of every door. Any areas that are worn, damaged, or missing should be replaced. If you still have air leaks, it may not be the weather stripping's fault. Door frames can settle and shift over time, causing the door to become crooked and gapped. Have a carpenter adjust your door, or try it yourself by adding small shims behind hinges.

WINDOWS Another hot spot for cold air is the gap around windows. A quick fix is to press "rope caulk" into any window joints that are leaking. This sticky stuff will stop the air flow, and it's not very noticeable. For particularly bad windows, you can tape clear plastic window film over the windows to seal them off, and use a hair dryer to smooth and tighten the plastic. This technique works well, but you won't be able to open the window without destroying the plastic.

CHIMNEYS If you have a fireplace, there should be a chimney flue damper. Check to see that it closes completely, as the warm air rising up the chimney can create a significant draft.

ELECTRICAL OUTLETS Feel for drafts around outlets, particularly on windy days. If you find a drafty socket or switch, turn off the power and remove the cover. Use a small amount of insulating spray foam around the electrical box, and at the point where the wires come through the box. DO NOT fill the box with foam or any other insulation. Replace the cover when done, and turn the power back on.

7 FIND A CHILLY LEAK

A few cracks around your windows can waste as much heat as one window left partially open all winter. A quick way to find these leaks is to move a burning stick of incense around your windows. The gentle flow of smoke will allow you to see the air movement and find the drafts. If you don't mind your home smelling like a yoga studio, this trick is for you.

❽ TUNE UP A FURNACE

Your furnace pumps the lifeblood of your home: heat. If the system isn't pumping efficiently, you could be wasting fuel and headed for a breakdown. Here are some steps to help you tune up your furnace.

STEP 1 Check the exterior of the furnace and the exhaust pipe. You don't want to see any black soot or residue (that means it's running poorly). Then turn on your heat and find the small port which lets you see the flames. If you have a propane or LP gas system, the flames should be steady and blue. If you have oil heat, the flames should be orange and strong. If the flames don't look right, follow the instruction manual to adjust the fuel-to-air mixture for optimal combustion.

STEP 2 Give it a good cleaning. Turn your thermostat down, turn the furnace off, and let it cool down fully. Once cool to the touch, open it up and vacuum out any dust, rust, or dirt.

STEP 3 Repair as needed. Some oil furnaces have insulation inside. Replace any that is damaged or falling down. In gas systems, you'll have a blower to move the heat through your duct work. If your unit has a belt-driven blower fan, check the belt for cracks and make sure it is under tension. A cracked or floppy drive belt won't last too long before it breaks, halting the flow of heat in your home. Replace worn or cracked belts, and tighten the tension on loose belts.

STEP 4 Replace the filters. Typical HVAC systems have air filters, which should be changed at the beginning of the season and monthly during the winter. Oil furnaces usually have an oil filter, which should also be changed out. This filter strains out rust and dirt from your oil tank, which could clog the nozzles that spray the fuel into the fire chamber.

❾ BEWARE OF CARBON MONOXIDE

Carbon monoxide poisoning occurs when the gas builds up in a person's bloodstream. As the CO level builds in the air, the body replaces the oxygen in your red blood cells with carbon monoxide. The lack of oxygen can cause serious tissue and organ damage, and even death.

My family felt the scary sensations of carbon monoxide poisoning due to a blocked stovepipe, and that was just one of many scenarios. Cracked heat manifolds within propane heating systems, clogged exhaust pipes in oil furnaces, and other malfunctions can also put your family at risk.

House fires are always a risk in combustion-based heating systems, and they warrant the use of several smoke alarms (in the kitchen, on

each level, and near your heating system). But the odorless, tasteless gas of carbon monoxide is also a threat. That's why it's important to have both smoke alarms and CO alarms in the home. You should always install at least one CO alarm near any woodstoves or indoor furnaces.

10 HEAT SAFELY

While there are many ways to heat your house, even during a power outage, there are also some ways that you shouldn't. Here are some common culprits.

FIREPLACE OR WOODSTOVE A few winters ago, the mesh over my family's woodstove pipe became clogged with soot, and carbon monoxide backed up into the room. We noticed we were becoming very irritable and tired—and then the CO alarm went off. We went outside, aired out the house, and thoroughly cleaned the pipe and screen.

BBQ GRILLS These are one of the most notorious sources of home carbon monoxide poisonings during power outages. Whether it's a propane or charcoal grill, don't try to heat the home with it. Leave that sucker outside in the snow. It's dangerous if brought indoors.

STOVES Using a camping stove indoors, or using your kitchen stove as a heater, are both horrible ideas. Both stoves are potential fire starters, and the camping stove could lead to CO poisoning in small spaces.

CANDLES A sea of lit candles may make for a sexy backdrop in a romantic comedy, but as a home (or room) heating option, candles are a horrific fire hazard. If you, a child, or a pet knock over a few candles, your carpets, drapes, and the room itself could be on fire within moments.

11 INSTALL A WOODSTOVE

You can install your own woodstove if you are handy with tools and you have someone to help you move it. Improper installations are one of the chief causes of heating-related house fires—so get it right.

FIND THE BEST SPOT The safest installation uses an existing fireplace and chimney; the stove sits on your fireproof hearth and the pipe goes up the chimney, passing through a shield that seals the flue. If you don't have a chimney, run the stovepipe through an exterior cinderblock or concrete wall—most basements have them.

BUILD A BASE The stove needs a fireproof base, like the bare concrete slab of your basement. Other flooring requires an insulated stove mat, or ceramic tile, marble, or slate installed over a cement underlayment board.

INSTALL THE STOVEPIPE Here's the hard part: safely cutting a hole through your wall. Use a hammer drill and large masonry bit to make a ring of holes slightly larger than the pipe's diameter, and carefully finish with a hammer and chisel. Use escutcheon rings and stove gasket rope to finish the pipe on both sides; measure, cut, and screw or rivet the pieces together; and use sturdy brackets and a rain cap. The pipe should be taller than the roof.

12 PICK A STOVE

Woodstoves offer certain advantages and are the best choice for "off-grid" applications. But pellet stoves and gas fireplace inserts have their own appeal. Here are some of the points for and against these three popular stove types.

	PROS	CONS
WOODSTOVE	• The best heat output • Needs no electricity • Cooking is possible on flat-topped stoves • You can cut your own fuel	• Messy and needs steady monitoring • The fuel can be laborious to cut, split, and handle • Most likely fire hazard
PELLET STOVE	• Self-sustaining • Good heat output • Easy cleanup • Low smoke output • Some can run on other fuel	• Requires electrical power • Useless during a power outage with no backup • Pellets may be hard to acquire during emergencies
GAS INSERT	• No smoke or mess • Push-button operation • Anyone can operate without any heavy lifting • Least likely fire hazard	• Puts out the least heat • Requires a propane or LP gas tank outside • Hard to cook over

13 CHOP WOOD

Chopping wood is an art form practiced since ancestral times. I love it! It's great exercise, and a handy way to get free firewood for home heating. But firewood cutting and splitting are not without their hazards. Follow these rules and you're more likely to finish your chores unscathed.

A. Buy the right tool for the firewood-busting job: a sharp splitting maul.

B. Set up a clear area to work, free of trip hazards and overhead obstructions.

C. Grab some gloves and goggles. Splinters in your hands and bark in your eyeballs aren't fun.

D. Select your biggest, widest log to act as a chopping block near your woodpile.

E. Set up your firewood pieces on the block one at a time, so that they stand upright and can remain stable.

F. Spread your feet a little wider than shoulder width. Swing your axe down through the firewood piece, bending a bit at the waist and intending to bury the axe blade in the chopping block. I find it helps to imagine that the wood isn't there at all.

G. Control your stroke so that any missed blows go into the ground or the chopping block—not your foot or shin.

14 BEAT THE ODDS

It would be bad enough to be trapped at home by ice, snow, or foul weather. But it would be even worse if your home caught fire while the rescue squad and fire department were hampered by the conditions. House fires occur often in winter, and the most common time of day for these fires is between 5:00 and 8:00 p.m. This may seem odd, until you learn the cause: cooking. According to the U.S. Fire Administration, fires during the winter season cause more than $2 billion USD worth of damage each year. Most of these events are preventable, so take steps to guard against fire this season.

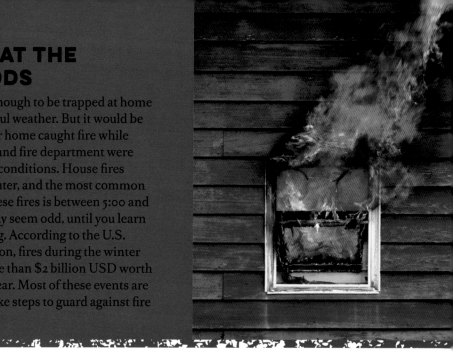

15 KILL A KITCHEN FIRE

Since cooking is the cause of most house fires, use extra care when preparing a hot meal for your snowed-in family. Apparently, it's not just my cooking that's dangerous. Remember, always get out of the house and call emergency services if you cannot control a fire.

DO	DON'T
Keep anything flammable (like paper towels and food packaging) at least 1 yard (1 m) away from your stove or cooktop.	Don't leave the kitchen when you're grilling, frying, or broiling food.
Keep a fire extinguisher handy in the kitchen, and make sure it is rated for grease fires.	Don't throw water, flour, or towels on a grease fire. Use baking soda or an extinguisher. You could also drop a large lid on the flaming pan to suffocate the flames.
Make sure that the oven, burners, and any appliances are turned off when you're done in the kitchen.	Don't try to pick up or move a flaming pan. You're likely to spread the fire and receive painful burns.

16 EXTINGUISH THE FLAME

Fire extinguishers can mystify us with their cryptic symbols and letters, but once you know the lingo, it's not hard to grasp. Keep your extinguisher accessible, and check the gauge before winter, making sure that the pressure needle is in the green zone.

 Puts out fires involving paper, plastics, cloth, wood, and rubber.

 Puts out fires involving grease, oil, gasoline, and oil-based paints.

 Puts out fires involving electrical equipment.

 Puts out fires involving animal or vegetable oils, or any other combustible cooking material.

17 MAKE A FIRE ESCAPE PLAN

This could be the most important survival plan that you and your family ever create. Design a fire escape plan and make sure it includes these guidelines.

RENDEZVOUS POINT An official meeting spot for your family.

DESIGNATED CALLER One family member who will go to a neighbor's house to call for help.

EXIT STRATEGY Plan for multiple escape possibilities from every room of the home.

Consider an escape ladder for upper stories.

STAY OUT PACT Never reenter a burning home for any reason; allow the firefighters to work.

PRACTICE SESSION Practice "stop, drop, and roll," low-crawling under smoke, and escaping the house in the dark.

18 ASSESS THE ICE

How do you know if an iced-over waterway is safe to traverse? Skating, ice fishing, hockey, and other ice sports get people outside in the winter, which is a great thing. Here are some ways to keep yourself safe and avoid ending up on thin ice—literally.

A. Never go out on the ice by yourself.

B. If you are ice fishing, or you are trying to rescue someone, wear a personal flotation device (PFD) under your winter clothes. Its insulation value will keep you warmer, too.

C. Never walk or drive on old or cloudy ice; only go out on clear, thick ice.

D. Carry ice picks in case you fall through. Purchase or make ones with floating handles and a rope to tether them together.

E. Keep the ice picks where they would be easy to reach if you do end up in the water.

F. 6-inch- (15-cm-) thick ice is probably safe for walking, skating, and ice fishing on foot.

G. 8-inch- (20-cm-) thick ice is probably safe for ATVs and snowmobiles.

H. 12-inch- (30-cm-) thick ice is probably safe for small cars or light pickups.

I. Remember that thawing spring ice is NEVER safe ice.

J. If in doubt, don't try it out.

19 SHOVEL YOUR ROOF

A snow-covered roof gives your home a gingerbread-like look and offers some temporary insulation value. But too much snow can lead to leaks, buckled roof trusses, or even a collapse. Here's what you need to know about roof shoveling.

GET A ROOF RAKE This long-handled tool is perfect for the roof snow removal job. You get to remain on solid ground and use the telescopic pole to scrape off snow. Just be careful of falling icicles, hard snow chunks, and overhead power lines.

DON'T DELAY As the snow piles up, so does the weight on your roof. One foot (0.3 m) of powdery snow may weigh only 3 pounds (1.4 kg) per square foot. But one foot of wet, heavy snow can weigh up to 21 pounds (9.5 kg), a dangerous burden for older roof systems. Rake the snow down before it reaches a dangerous mass.

FORGET THE GARDEN HOSE Some well-meaning folks break out the garden hose to spray the snow off their roof. Bad idea! The snow will absorb the water and increase the weight on the roof. Water spraying has been responsible for not only the destruction of roofs on single-family homes but also on large industrial buildings.

BEAT THE ICE DAM Even if your roof is strong, it's a good idea to remove the snow before it causes ice damming—when ice forms under the snow and causes the roof to leak.

20 SHOVEL SMART

For those who are able, shoveling snow is an excellent opportunity for exercise and a welcome reprieve from cabin fever. It's also a prime opportunity to wreck your back and give yourself a heart attack. Every snowstorm profits the chiropractors. Don't be another winter statistic.

LAYER UP Wear breathable, loose layers of clothing, so you can peel off one layer at a time.

STRETCH OUT Stretch your back, legs, and arms before you start, to prevent injury.

BOOT IT Pull on a good pair of boots. For traction (and for your toes), wear waterproof boots.

STAY ON PACE Keep up with the snow rather than waiting for it to stop. It may be more trips, but the work will be easier.

PUSH IT Act like a snowplow, not a forklift. Pushing the snow to the side takes less effort than lifting it.

HYDRATE Drink lots of water. This is a major workout, and it should be treated like one.

STOP! Stop and call 911 if you have unusual shortness of breath, pain, or a heavy feeling in your chest, neck, or arms; if you're dizzy or feeling faint; or if you experience nausea and vomiting.

21 WINTERIZE YOUR GARDEN

The deep, cold sleep between fall and spring is an inevitable part of the gardening cycle. Use the following tricks to help your perennials survive and prepare the garden for planting in the springtime.

MULCH IT Apply a generous layer of mulch to everything. Cover your garden beds with wood chips. Cover your strawberry bed with straw. This covering provides a microclimate which can save your plants by insulating them.

BURY YOUR POTS Potted plants are very vulnerable to freezing. Bury these in the ground to protect the roots, or at least bury the pots in a pile of mulch.

WATER THE SOIL Before the ground freezes, soak it deeply with water (if your fall rains were lacking). This extra moisture can keep plants alive during midwinter dry spells. Leave winter veggies in place. Carrots, garlic, parsnips, and other root crops can be left in the ground to sweeten, and dug as needed in early winter. Place markers so that you can find these buried treasures when there's snow on the ground.

CLEAR OUT THE SKELETONS Dispose of dead tomato plants, squash stalks, and any other deceased vegetation that could be harboring insect eggs or pathogens.

PRUNE THE BERRIES Give blackberries and raspberries a late fall pruning. Trim back bushes that bear fruit in the fall aggressively. For summer-bearing bushes, just remove dead canes and the ones that have already produced.

PLANT SOME WOODY PLANTS Early winter is a great time to plant trees, shrubs, and vines. The semi-dormant plants can focus on root growth over the winter, without the stresses of trying to grow leaves.

PREP THE DIRT Till your garden beds and apply a layer of aged manure or compost, which will break down over the winter and enrich the soil for next year.

22 CARE FOR CRITTERS

It's your job to make sure the animals in your life stay safe and healthy in the winter. But should your cat play in the snow? Does your dog need boots? How do you keep your cows from being killed by a deep freeze? Here's how to prepare your beasts for a wintry blast.

COMPANION ANIMALS Our pets may think it's fun to bound through the snow—or they might be terrified. You know your pets best, so read their cues. Buy a pet sweater for animals with short coats. Invest in some dog boots if their paws become tender or bleed. Feed them a little extra to compensate for the cold temperatures. And remember that it's not OK to leave dogs and cats out in the cold, even cold-climate breeds, unless adequate shelter is available.

LIVESTOCK If you have a farm or just some backyard chickens, you know that winter can be a very tough season for livestock. Even hardy animals can be killed by the cold. Cattle, horses, sheep, goats, and similar grazers will need extra feed to generate the metabolic heat to stay warm out in the elements. Buy extra hay in late summer or fall, before the prices go up or the local supply runs out. Pigs and chickens will need extra food, too. Even hives of bees may need some extra feeding during long periods of cold, or you'll find a box of dead bees in the spring. All livestock will need plenty of water, so invest in a heating element to keep their water trough from icing over.

23 10 EMERGENCY USES FOR SNOW

In the form of a whiteout storm or a vehicle-trapping drift, snow can often place people in deadly situations. But strangely enough, that same snow is also a versatile and useful substance that can help you in a number of situations. Here are my top ten favorite ways to use snow for survival.

SHELTER Snow can be turned into many survival shelters. From igloos and quinzees to snow caves and tree wells, a shelter of snow can mean survival on a sub-freezing night.

WATER Melt it into a liquid for safe hydration—make sure to give your newfound water a boil if the snow is old and potentially contaminated by animals.

SIGNAL Stomp out a giant "SOS" or "V" in a snowy clearing. Use charcoal or other substances to color the snow.

FOOD PRESERVATION Use snow to keep your foods from spoiling. Pack snow into coolers or simply bury your food in it. Mark it well for easy retrieval.

TRACKING HEAVEN Even a novice can see details in the white stuff. Learn which species live nearby, and follow their wanderings.

COLD PACK Snow makes a great cold pack for injuries. Just fill a plastic bag with snow, wrap it in some cloth, and hold it on sprains and strains.

SNOW CONE Unmelted snow isn't a water source, but it is a great snack. One delicious Native American treat is maple syrup drizzled over snow.

TRAIL MARKERS Create temporary trail markers with pylons of snow. Use colorants, if possible, to help you spot the white pillars.

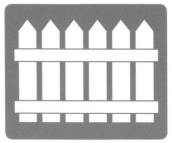

TRAPPER KEEPER Build snow funnels and fencing at your trap sites. These walls, holes, paths, and other structures will direct your prey to just the right spot.

TOILET PAPER SUBSTITUTE Snow that packs into a good snowball is suitable for wiping. It does it all: melts, scours, washes, and absorbs.

24 DRESS THE PART

Clothing selection is a critical part of preparing for any outdoor trip, particularly in winter. Anticipate the worst weather extremes you could face, and then multiply them. Prepare from head to toe with careful clothing, footwear, and outerwear selections. For most winter and cold-climate living, dress in layers of material that are made from wool or synthetic fibers. These materials will not hold moisture the way cotton does (and wet cotton clothing is a bad thing, conducting your body heat away and paving the way for hypothermia).

For cold and wet weather, dress in loose layers with a synthetic layer underneath.

This means that your socks, underwear, long johns, and other base-layer clothing should be made of polypropylene, nylon, rayon, or another synthetic fabric. Wool is fine for this layer, too—but it's itchy. Either wool or synthetic can make up your middle layer of shirts, sweaters, pants, and hats. Outer layers like coats, jackets, and rainwear should be warm with a breathable (yet waterproof) synthetic outer layer like Gore-Tex. Select outerwear with hoods and lots of pockets to hold spare gear. Top things off with very warm gloves, headwear, sunglasses or goggles in bright snowy conditions, and some spare clothing—just in case.

BASE	MIDDLE	OUTER
Socks, underwear, long johns, should be made polypropylene, nylon, rayon, or another synthetic fabric.	Wool or synthetic fabrics can make up your middle layer of shirts, sweaters, pants, and hats.	Outer layers should be warm with a breathable, waterproof, synthetic outer layer like Gore-Tex.

25 COLOR CODE IT

You should also consider color in your clothing selections. Bright colors can signal for help and increase your visibility, so even if you want to blend into the environment with camouflage, keep some bright items on hand. A blaze orange or red bandanna in your coat pocket can serve many purposes besides acting as a signal flag.

Be ready to change your clothing to suit the changing conditions around you. Some basic layers can keep you comfortable in cool weather. As the temperature drops and the precipitation starts, you'd better have the rest of this gear to stay warm and dry.

	BASE LAYER	MID-LAYER	COAT	HAT	GLOVES	SHOES
COLD RAIN	Synthetic T-shirt	Waterproof rain pants, warm shirt	Gore-Tex shell with fleece liner	Wear a big waterproof hat over your jacket hood	Waterproof gloves	Waterproof boots—plus synthetic socks
FREEZING RAIN	Synthetic T-shirt and long john bottoms	Waterproof rain pants, warm shirt	Gore-Tex shell with fleece liner	Waterproof hat over hood	Insulated waterproof gloves	Waterproof boots and synthetic socks
CLEAR AND COLD	Synthetic T-shirt and long john bottoms	Wool shirt or sweater, heavy wool or canvas pants	Down coat or parka	You bet!	Insulated gloves	Insulated snow boots or mukluks, wool socks
SNOW	Full set of long johns, top and bottom	Snow pants, sweater	Down coat or parka	A beanie works well; a balaclava is better	Insulated gloves	Insulated snow boots or mukluks, wool socks
-20 BELOW	Full set of long johns, top and bottom	Long-sleeved shirt, hoodie, and insulated pants	Light, down coats rated for very cold weather	Warm wool, shearling, or high-tech synthetics	When it's really cold, mittens are better	Warm, waterproof, nonslip soles—plus wool socks
SEVERE WINDS	Full set of long johns, top and bottom	Insulated coveralls and a thick hoodie	A windproof outer shell for windy conditions	A very warm hat that can't be blown off your head	A must; high winds lead to fast frostbite	Insulated boots or mukluks, wool socks

27 LAY ON THE LAYERS

Wearing your clothing in layers is usually the best way to create dead air space around your body, but be aware that there are a few ways this insulation strategy can fail. Be smart!

DON'T DO IT WRONG

Skip the tight clothes. Garments that are too small will compress the insulation under them and diminish their insulating value.

Omit the cotton. A great fabric for daytime adventures in hot and arid climates, cotton holds moisture for a long time and helps cool you down. This makes it a terrible fabric for cold-climate activities. If it's cold enough for long johns, they shouldn't be cotton—ever.

DO IT RIGHT

Dress in loose layers. These work efficiently and are easy to remove if you overheat.

Select zippered garments. Coats and jackets with front zippers (or even armpit zippers) are excellent for helping you to regulate your body temperature. Unzip to cool down, and zip up when you're feeling chilly again.

Choose wool and synthetic items, especially for base layers (long johns). These are breathable and they don't hold on to moisture like some other fabrics.

28 INVEST WISELY

Since you usually get what you pay for, do some research into where you should spend your winter clothing budget and where you can scrimp. A few well-chosen items might last for years, saving you money in the long run. It always pays to do your research before you start dropping money on seasonal gear. Consult buyer's guides and outdoor magazine reviews. Read product reviews online. Ask your friends about their gear, and how they like it. And finally, ask the pros. Talk to guides, outfitters, and any other outdoor professionals to see what gear they recommend and what brands and items they would avoid. The right items can last for years, if you put some money in up front and treat them right. Here are some places where you should really do your homework.

COATS Coats should be warm, durable, and have sturdy zippers and plenty of pockets. Hoods are a necessity, as are backup closures like buttons.

PANTS Pants should have reinforced knees, insulation, and be made of tough fabric.

BOOTS Boots should be waterproof, well-insulated, and have an aggressive tread pattern. They should not produce blisters or be too constricting. Many people buy the next size up so that they can comfortably wear two pairs of socks underneath.

 # CARE FOR YOUR CLOTHES

Don't destroy your expensive gear trying to get it clean. Some winter clothing and outerwear choices require very particular handling when wet, dirty, or salty, or prior to storage.

WOOL COATS, SWEATERS, AND PANTS

Wool is great for cold conditions, especially in wet climates.

A. Don't wash wool items unless they're very dirty. Use a lint or suede brush for a quick cleaning.

B. "Hand wash only" garments can usually go in your washing machine's hand-wash or wool cycle with cool water.

C. For a real hand wash, use a wool-friendly detergent and lukewarm water. Soak for 3 to 5 minutes and rub very gently, then rinse in cool water. Never use hot water or bleach on wool.

D. To dry wool garments, press them between dry towels. Then lay them flat until dry. Don't hang until completely dry, as the shape will distort. Wash and dry before storage, as moths love dirty wool more than clean wool.

DOWN JACKETS, VESTS, AND SLEEPING BAGS

Down is perfect for cold, dry conditions, but its insulating properties reduce greatly when wet.

A. Hand wash or use a front-loading washer. Top-loading machines can cause damage.

B. Use a loft-restoring, down-friendly detergent, available in outdoor sports stores.

C. Rinse the item twice, making sure all of the detergent is removed.

D. Dry it slowly with low heat. High heat can damage the down garment.

E. Air drying isn't recommended, as it takes a long time and doesn't fluff the down feathers.

F. Store these items loose, never packed tightly, or they will lose some of their loft.

WATERPROOF, TECHNICAL FABRIC CLOTHING AND OUTERWEAR

Gore-Tex and similar fabrics are waterproof yet breathable materials, specially designed for the outdoors. Their DWR (durable water repellent) treatment causes water to roll off the surface. This treatment can wear out with heavy use and be brought back with the proper soap and procedure.

1. Use a soap designed for these garments, like a Gore-Tex revitalizing wash. Don't use powder or liquid detergents, surfactants, or bleaches, which harm the DWR treatment.

2. Machine wash in a front loader, if possible, on a warm permanent press setting.

3. Rinse the garment twice to remove oils and soap, then line dry or tumble dry on warm.

GO TOWARD THE LIGHT

The beauty of a headlamp is that it puts the light you need right in front of you, yet it leaves both hands free to work. Gone are the days of juggling a heavy flashlight or lantern while you peer under the hood of your truck, head into the wilderness, or explore a crittery crawlspace. Not all headlamps are alike, however, so be choosy in your search.

BATTERY POWER Look for a headlamp that offers a nice long battery life. LED bulbs allow standard AA or AAA batteries to crank out over 100 hours of light in some models. This is an amazing development, especially compared to the battery-gobbling flashlights of the '80s and '90s.

WATER RESISTANCE Your headlamp should also have some margin of waterproofing. You may need it in the rain, or in other conditions where it may get wet. Waterproofing can save the device from water damage, and keep your dark world illuminated.

BONUS FEATURES A nice side feature for your headlamp is an optional setting that activates a bright incandescent bulb. LED bulbs can be very bright at short range, but the incandescent bulb can produce a strong beam that can reach out some distance. This is perfect for inspecting the shadowy creature rustling the bushes 100 feet (30 m) into the black forest (it was just your dog, by the way).

Always pack some spare batteries with your headlamp. Batteries are always at risk of leaking, or the lamp could get bumped into "on" mode during storage and drain the supply. One way to avoid the latter, if you're storing your lamp for a long period of time, is to slip a piece of paper between the battery and the metal port. It'll prevent a connection in case of accidental jostling, and guard against any battery drain.

COOL TOOLS
HEADLAMP

Favored by miners in historic times, and spelunkers more recently, the outdoor sports community finally began to embrace this hands-free lighting option about 25 years ago. Since then, there's been a boom in available brands and features. Whether you're working on your furnace in the dark, creepy basement, trying to fix a meal during a winter power outage, or simply walking the dog in the evening, a headlamp is one of those tools that you won't know how you lived without.

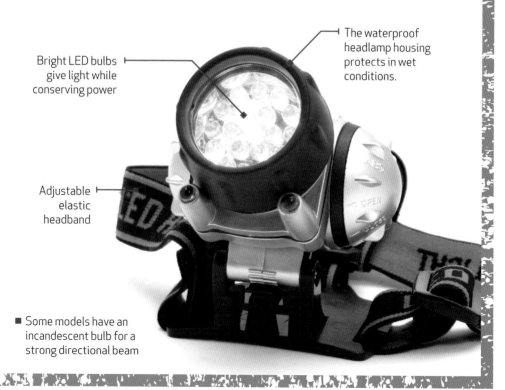

The waterproof headlamp housing protects in wet conditions.

Bright LED bulbs give light while conserving power

Adjustable elastic headband

■ Some models have an incandescent bulb for a strong directional beam

32 GIRD YOUR GARAGE

Do you have what you need to get your garage winter-ready and keep your car running in all conditions? Winter is a tough season for automobiles, and the cold can take a toll. Here are some key items to stock before the season sets in.

 ANTIFREEZE A jug of pre-mixed antifreeze can be added to your coolant if the level drops due to a crack or leak in the system. Don't add plain water, as it can freeze and burst cooling components.

 WASHER FLUID A bottle of low-temp washer fluid replenishes the reservoir from the frequent washing that the road spray requires.

 MOTOR OIL The numbers and letters on the bottle refer to viscosity (thickness) at different temperatures. "W" refers to winter—a 5W oil is typically recommended. for winter, and you'll want a 5W-20 or 5W-30 for lower temperatures.

 STORAGE SHELVING Grab some shelving for your garage; as the snow and ice melt off your vehicle and puddle on the floor, it's nice to keep your supplies and belongings out of the mess.

 MOTION-SENSITIVE LIGHTING If you don't have an automatic light on your garage-door opener, install a motion-sensing light source. The short winter days can mean leaving in the dark and returning in the dark.

33 WINTERIZE YOUR RIDE

There are some crucial tasks for every car owner to complete before the mercury drops. Some of them are easy to do on your own and some may require a trip to the shop, but remember that you can save a lot of money, time, and sanity by taking some preventative measures before the cold snap hits. Consider this a pre-winter checklist for winterizing your vehicle.

GO WITH A PRO

☐ If it's time for a tune-up, get it done before winter. The cold can worsen existing problems in starting, idling, and performance.

☐ Clean, flush, and refill the antifreeze in the cooling system. This doesn't have to be done every year, but if you're going to do it, do it before winter.

☐ Get a battery and charging system checkup. Cold weather demands much more current from a battery. To add insult to injury, the cold prevents the battery from producing the normal amount of energy.

DIY

☐ Start your engine and let it warm up. Once hot, check your heaters and defrosters, which pull heat from the engine to warm the cabin and windshield.

☐ Check your wiper blades for any sign of wear and tear. If in doubt, replace them with new blades.

☐ Begin topping off your washer fluid with low-temp, cold-weather washer fluid.

☐ Make sure your exterior and interior lights all work.

☐ Check your tire tread depth and tire pressure. Bald tires are very dangerous in slick conditions, and tire pressure can decrease from the cold. Continue to check your tires and tire pressure several times a month through the winter.

☐ One bonus task: Keep the gas tank at least half full at all times. This acts as a safety net for your winter travels, and may decrease the chance of moisture freezing in the lines.

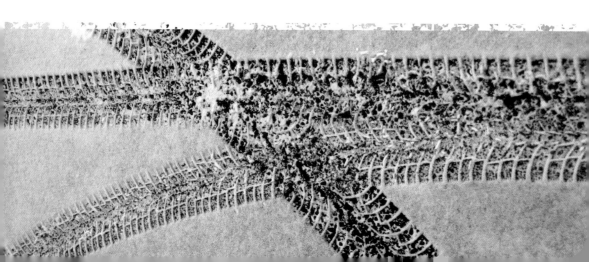

34 DRIVE IN THE SNOW

Taking the car out in the winter, either for fun or for work, is not the same as driving in other seasons. Extreme cold or a few flurries may not constitute an emergency, but they do affect the rules of the road. These driving tricks will help you to keep your car between the ditches and with the greasy side down.

WATCH YOUR SPEED Drive slower, because speed is one of the chief causes of winter driving accidents. Just because you're driving a four-wheel-drive tank doesn't mean you can fly.

EASY DOES IT Accelerate and decelerate slowly and gently. Don't jerk the wheel when turning. Quick movements often lead to loss of control.

DON'T STOP! As we all learned in fourth grade, objects already in motion tend to stay in motion, so if you're going up a hill, don't stop. If you do, and it's slippery, chances are that you'll get stuck. Use your momentum to keep going.

PUMP THE BRAKES It's important to know what kind of brakes your vehicle has. If you drive an older vehicle that doesn't have anti-lock brakes, "pump" the brakes to maintain control when stopping.

SPACE IT OUT Leave plenty of room to stop between you and other cars. Normal following distance on dry pavement is about four seconds between vehicles. In winter weather, you should increase that space to ten seconds.

JUST STAY HOME If you're concerned about the safety of the roads and you don't absolutely need to be somewhere, just stay home.

35 USE TIRE CHAINS

Tire chains (or snow chains) are hardly a new invention. Due to their destructive impact on road surfaces, chains are not legal everywhere, but when allowed and warranted, they make a huge difference in traction. Only use tire chains when the road surface has a layer of compacted snow or ice on top of it. If you can see the road surface, chains are probably prohibited and quality snow tires should be sufficient.

GET THE FIT Purchase the correct size chains for your tires; a proper fit is vital to safety and function. It also pays to install and adjust them before you actually need them. The middle of a blizzard is an awful time to try installing tire chains for the first time.

INSTALL CORRECTLY Only install chains on the drive wheels. If you are driving a four-wheel-drive vehicle, you'll need chains for each wheel. But two wheel drive vehicles only need two sets. Don't deflate the air in your tires to install tire chains. The correctly sized tire chain, properly fitted and adjusted, will go over your properly inflated tires.

AVOID BREAKAGE Speed and dry pavement are the two main reasons that properly sized and installed chains break. Keep your speed between 20 to 30 mph (30 to 50 kph). You'd be crazy to drive faster in a blizzard anyway. Stop and take the chains off when you finally reach dry pavement.

36 PARK AT YOUR PERIL

Finding a place to park isn't always easy when the snowplows are out. Vacant parking spots become snow piles, parallel parking gets harder, and cars can even be buried by well-meaning plow drivers.

Even though it may mean slogging through the snow and slush, it's safer to park in lots and garages. On the street, plows may cover the car in snow and ice, the plow blade could sideswipe your vehicle, and there's that terrible frozen hump of snow between the plowed street and the parked vehicle. It might as well be the Himalayas to a smaller, two-wheel-drive car. Of course, the safest way to circumvent the snowy parking nightmare is to ask a buddy for a ride, and leave your car where it sits until the snow melts away.

37 PLAN FOR DELAYS

A scant snowfall just turned your typical 30-minute commute into two hours of white-knuckle traffic. One of the best ways to survive your commute is to plan ahead for weather delays. The next time wintry precipitation is predicted during rush hour, pull these rabbits out of your furry hat.

BEAT THE RUSH Leave home early, before the weather event or before the traffic gets bad. If you can't start work early, you can at least choose where to spend your time. Would you rather be stuck on the highway for an hour, or sitting in the cozy coffee shop by the office?

CHOOSE ALTERNATE ROUTES There's always another way to get to your destination. If you find that alternate routes are passable, you could take a more circuitous path to work. There will probably be more stoplights, lower speed limits, and other hindrances—but as long as you're moving, it feels like progress. This change of pace can be a nice alternative to staying on the sluggish highway.

USE FLEX TIME If your employer is the understanding type, you may be able to change your work hours on the fly. Go in later, after the roads are clear and the traffic has dwindled. Stay late and miss the evening rush hour, too. Better yet, work from home and dodge the madness completely.

38 KEEP YOUR COOL

Slogging to work in the slush and fighting your way home through the frost isn't so bad if you can keep your spirits up. But that's (much) easier said than done, and rush hour tends to bring out the worst in everyone. For most of us, traveling in bad weather—whether commuting or road tripping—raises our blood pressure, lowers our patience, and frazzles our nerves. Check yourself before you wreck yourself with these great anger management aids.

	TECHNIQUE
MUSIC	Soothing tunes like classical music, holiday music, folk music, and any other calming melodies can take the edge off your stressful winter trek.
HOT BEVERAGES	Who could be infuriated by other drivers while sipping hot cocoa? Some drinks are especially sweet, nourishing, and comforting. Skip the coffee and pick something calming.
FOOD	You don't want to drive around "hangry" (a deplorable combination of hungry and angry). Keep some of your favorite snacks in the car to give you a more comforting commute to work in the morning and help you unwind on your way home.
AUDIO	Audiobooks and other forms of intellectual entertainment can make the hours seem like minutes. It's almost impossible to be possessed by the demon of road rage during Morgan Freeman's stirring reading of *The Shawshank Redemption*.

39 DODGE THE DANGERS

The psychology and motivations of drivers can be clearly seen in the rate of accidents on certain days and at specific times. Fridays average out as the most accident-prone commute day, and the reason seems to boil down to one simple factor: Drivers are thinking about the weekend ahead and not the road in front of them. According to the Insurance Institute for Highway Safety, the most dangerous time to be on the roads is between 5:00 p.m. and 7:00 p.m. as people are rushing to get home for the evening. Of course, other factors come into play when the weather takes a bad turn. For example, the first day after a snowstorm is statistically more dangerous than the day of the storm (because most people stay home or use more caution during the storm). And an ice event can send everyone skidding into each other. Increase your odds of staying safe by employing these four commute safety tips.

STOP TEXTING Not only is it illegal in most areas, it distracts you from the road.

WATCH YOUR SPEED Driving more slowly gives you the time to react to the sudden moves made by other cars. Give yourself both the time and distance to react.

LEAD BY EXAMPLE Use your turn signal, leave room between cars, maintain a steady speed, and follow the rules. You might just inspire the drivers around you to do the same.

JOIN THE WATCH Check your mirrors often. Watch the two cars in front of you. This allows you to react at the same time as the car in front of you does and therefore prevent the most common automobile accident: rear-ending in traffic.

40 POP A WINTER WHEELIE

The dangers to motorcyclists really stack up in the winter. As if the cold tires and slick pavement weren't enough, now you have to face the risk of hypothermia and frostbite. If you have to take your bike out in the cold, get yourself and the bike ready well in advance.

AFTERMARKET EQUIPMENT FOR WINTER RIDING The most basic cold-weather adaptations help to block the roaring wind. Handguards and a generous windscreen can limit the cold air that is hitting your body, keeping you warmer. They may look ugly, but they're

worth it. Heated grips can also make a big difference for frozen hands.

DRESS FOR SURVIVAL Your normal riding leathers have no business on a winter ride, unless you've lost a ton of weight and you're wearing them over many layers. Leather has no insulation value, so layer up by starting with a base layer of synthetic material, wool socks, and a neck warmer. Add wool pants and a sweater, or synthetic sweats, and then a wind-cutting Gore-Tex suit, winter riding gloves, and insulated Gore-Tex boots.

41 WINTERIZE YOUR BIKE

Winter can be cruel to both bike and rider. Here's what you can do to put your machine into storage.

CLEAN IT Give the bike a thorough wash, and wax all the metal areas to avoid rust.

PARK INDOORS If you don't have a heated garage, find a place protected from rain and rodents.

DEAL WITH FUEL Add a fuel stabilizer to a full tank and ride a bit; this works best with fuel injectors. Or drain the fuel and run the engine dry to prevent varnishing. Spray the inside of metal fuel tanks with WD-40 or another rust inhibitor.

CHANGE THE OIL Change it before you park the bike, and again before you begin riding.

Moisture from condensation gets into the oil and compromises it. Oil's cheap; new bearings aren't.

PREP THE ENGINE Ride briefly to warm the bike, then remove the spark plugs and squirt the holes with engine oil (25cc). Turn the bike over with the plugs out (put the bike in gear, raise the rear wheel, and spin it a few times). Replace the plugs.

PROTECT THE BATTERY Disconnect it and store it where it won't freeze. Or, put it on a trickle charger.

SAVE YOUR TIRES Put the bike on stands to get both tires off the ground.

USE ANTIFREEZE With a liquid-cooled bike, use a hydrometer to check out the cooling system.

SHIELD YOUR PIPES Keep critters out with plugs or a sheet of plastic.

42 CYCLE IN THE SNOW

If you bike to work or school, a little snow can throw a wrench in your cycling. You'll need warm clothing and some specialized gear.

RIDER GEAR Head and neck coverings are musts. Even on a still day, your movement simulates wind—and wind chill. A cycling headband under your helmet is great, to keep warm without overheating. A neck gaiter can be pulled up over your face if needed, and your jacket and pants should be windproof and breathable. To prevent being soaked at the skin, wear a breathable synthetic base layer (no cotton). Invest in some lobster gloves for warmth and lever control. Finish off with waterproof boots that have rubber soles for adequate control while pedaling.

BIKE GEAR The shorter daylight hours of winter mean more riding in the dark. Use a front white light and a rear red light on your bike. Carry a spare set of lights as a backup. Get your bike ready for slippery surfaces by swapping out your slick road tires with nubby ones on days with any accumulated snow or sleet. The better grip of these tires will give you better handling and more control. But make sure that your frame has enough clearance when buying winter tires.

43 RUN IN THE SNOW

If you're a serious runner, you're not going to let a little snow stop you. But you do need to be prepared for the harsh conditions.

GEAR UP Repurpose and layer other sporting apparel to create a warm, comfy running outfit. If you're willing to splurge, recent advances in technical clothing can save you from trying to figure out what to do with the extra clothes you've peeled off after warming up. Your running shoes should also be engineered for winter—well-ventilated summer shoes can lead to cold feet, or even frostbitten toes. Choose running shoes with aggressive tread, some insulation, and a Gore-Tex outer fabric to keep your feet dry when you hit a patch of slush. Keep your ears covered, and wear gloves, too.

EAT FOR THE COLD There's no shortage of conflicting advice on winter sports nutrition, but everyone can agree on the need for extra calories. Each breath of frozen air chills your throat and lungs, which must be reheated by the fires of your metabolism. Whatever you eat now as a runner, consider doubling it. This may seem like a lot, but it's not uncommon to blow through 1,000 calories an hour in extreme cold conditions.

AVOID INJURY Run on fresh snow with lots of traction (not the packed, icy stuff) to minimize slips and falls, and be aware of the look and feel of frostbite. Finally, know when to skip the workout for the sake of your health. Running in a whiteout could cause you to run off course and become lost—or run into something dangerous.

44 WALK THE DOG

As every canine lover knows, dog walking is necessary for your companion, and that doesn't change with the advent of winter. They need to exercise and do their business, and keeping up with the daily walk will acclimate you both to the rigors of winter. Get a warm pup coat for cold-natured dogs, and invest in dog boots for trudging through salt or de-icers. And if you're snowed in, train your pudgy pooch to walk on a treadmill—or break your own rules by playing ball in the house.

45 JOIN THE TEAM

So many people use the cold weather as an excuse for laziness and lethargy. For those who find that their motivation comes and goes during the season, set yourself up for success by joining a team or group that centers around a healthy activity. This way, you'll have people nagging you if you don't show up or if you don't play hard, and you'll still get your blood pumping (which, in turn, helps beat the winter blues). Here are just a few enjoyable winter sports options.

HOCKEY Winter means ice, and ice means hockey. Find an amateur team near you and show up for tryouts.

CURLING Curling is another icy favorite in many northern parts of the world.

ICE SKATING Skate for speed or skate as a form of expression. You could even make your own rink in the backyard (see item 52).

SKIING AND SNOWSHOEING What better way to take advantage of the snow than to explore it on snowshoes or cross-country skis?

INDOOR SPORTS If your blood's feeling thin, pick up a lively indoor sport. There are clubs for everything: football, the other football, basketball, rugby, lacrosse, you name it!

SWIMMING Check out your local health club, find an indoor heated pool, and take up swimming.

SHOOTING It's never too cold to shoot!

46 10 EMERGENCY USES FOR OIL

Lard, vegetable oil, and the grease from a can of tuna fish—these household oils may not seem very important as survival items, but they can play a surprising variety of roles in emergencies. While oil is usually most important as a calorie source, even rancid grease can prove useful. Here are ten reasons to add oil to your winter survival stash.

CALORIES Fats are the densest source of calories, and every calorie counts. Add a little oil to other foods to spike up their calorie content.

RUST-PROOFING Protect knives, tools, and other metal objects with a light coat of oil. Only use food-grade oil on your cooking surfaces.

MEDICINES Healing plants can be dried and soaked in oil to create salves and balms. Try chickweed for itching and comfrey for wounds.

PRESERVATION Vegetables, fish, and mushrooms can be preserved for a brief time in edible oil.

LIGHT Add a cotton twine wick to a can of oil, and you have a primitive grease lamp for emergency lighting.

SOAP Oil can be blended with lye and water, stirred until slushy, and then set aside for aging to create some homemade soap.

LOTION Dry, winter-cracked skin can get a healing boost from a light rub of oil. This helps to keep moisture in so that healing can begin.

FIRE HELPER Add a little oil to damp wood, charcoal, paper, cardboard, or any other flammables to help them burn better and longer.

LUBRICANT Cooking oil can pass for chainsaw bar oil, friction fire socket lube, folding knife pin lubricant, and many other uses.

FUEL Unused cooking oil can be turned into biodiesel with the right mixture of lye and methanol. Use caution and mix chemicals outdoors.

47 NOTE THE SIGNS OF SAD

Seasonal affective disorder (also known as SAD) is a form of depression tied to the changes in daylight hours and seasons. For many, SAD becomes part of their annual health cycle—beginning and ending around the same times (commonly in the fall and through the winter months). This debilitating condition can cause a wide range of symptoms; here's how to tell if you or a loved one is affected (vs. just feeling a bit blue).

LOSS OF ENERGY Some feel invigorated by the cool air of autumn, but if that doesn't apply—especially if you experience a heavy feeling in your limbs—pay attention to your energy level and seek help if it continues to drop.

MOODINESS Being cranky from time to time is normal. Having wild mood swings and irritability without an obvious reason is not. Pay attention to feedback from friends and family, as you may miss the cues yourself. Difficulty getting along with other people and being overly sensitive to rejection are frequent hallmarks of SAD.

OVERSLEEPING If you're normally OK on eight hours a night, but begin routinely sleeping ten or more hours, it can be a sign of SAD.

WEIGHT GAIN A greater appetite, weight gain, and cravings for high-carb foods are additional signs of SAD.

48

FLIP THE SWITCH

While we may never know the specific causes of seasonal affective disorder, there are some factors that seem to be guilty culprits. These may include your circadian rhythm (biological clock), serotonin levels, and melatonin (which affects sleep and mood), all of which can deviate from the norm with the changing seasons. Here are some of things you can do to fight back against SAD.

BASK IN THE LIGHT Light therapy boxes are lamps that mimic sunlight, using bright bulbs in different wavelengths than standard light bulbs. The average exposure involves sitting by the light for a half hour each day to reset your body's circadian rhythms.

RISE AND SHINE Set a sleep schedule and stick to it. Plan to go to sleep and wake up at the same time each day, and if you need help in the morning, consider a "dawn simulator" clock. These produce gradually increasing light as well as an alarm. I use one year-round because it wakes me up gently—with realistic bird songs that get louder as you lie there snoozing.

EXERCISE YOUR DEMONS A proven mood booster, winter exercise is a must, so hit the gym, elliptical, or indoor pool. In addition to the feel-good chemicals that get dumped into your bloodstream during a good workout, your physical effort will burn extra calories, helping to offset the SAD-associated weight gain you may be experiencing (see left).

GET OUTSIDE Outdoor exercise is one of the most helpful DIY remedies for SAD. I know it's rough outside in the winter, and the last thing you want to do is go out in it, but the facts don't lie—so suit up for the cold and make the best of it. Even if it's just your face sticking out of the bundles of clothing, you're still getting some light in your eyes and on your skin. The latter allows your body to produce some much-needed vitamin D, and the former helps with your circadian rhythm.

49

TALK TO YOUR DOCTOR

Professional help is the best treatment for any form of depression. Simple treatments for SAD can involve light therapy (phototherapy), psychotherapy, and prescription medications. Seek a doctor if you're concerned that a loved one's behavior points to more than just the winter blues. Look for all the usual signs of depression: feeling down multiple days in a row, losing interest in activities, a change in sleeping or eating, or relying on substances for comfort.

50

GRAB THE TOOL OF WARMTH

OK, it's a bit of a stretch to count a sock as a tool—unless there's a doorknob in it and you're using it for self-defense. Even so, I still count a good pair of warm socks as the best tools to keep your feet protected and warm. After purchasing countless hiking socks, work-boot socks, winter socks, and other hard-use foot coverings, I have tried everything to find a sock that can stand up to my abusive feet and their winter environment. But then I got a pair of Point 6 socks (see opposite) and wore them off and on for a year—and I continue to be impressed. They are still soft, still warm, and still don't have any holes in them—a real feat. A good pair of socks is a great investment in cold-weather comfort—and in guarding all your toes from frostbite.

51
BANISH FOUL ODORS

The right pair of feet can turn any pair of socks into eye-watering stinkers. To start, try to avoid brands with a high synthetic content, and then keep things reek-free with a wash that includes distilled vinegar, which is murder on the bacteria hiding in your socks. Just 1 cup (0.25 l) of vinegar in your laundry load should banish most odors. For an especially awful pair, do a pre-wash soak in straight vinegar.

COOL TOOLS
POINT 6 SOCKS

Point 6 is named after 98.6° F, the human body's optimal core temperature—and these socks are one more strategy to help keep you there. They're made from merino wool, which naturally regulates body temperature by feeling cool when you've warmed up, and feeling warm when you're cold. The reason these socks are so tough (as well as warm) is the quality of the wool, which is crafted with some high-tech spinning techniques that create a compact spun yarn with more merino fibers per inch than any other wool fibers. This yarn can then be knitted into soft wool socks without the dreaded scratchiness or bulk of their traditional counterparts. Here are some of the other fine points of the Point 6 sock:

Compact yarn reduces loose fibers, which lead to pilling and untimely wear

Warm, yet prevents overheating

Precise anatomical fit for both men's and women's feet

These fibers stay warm, even when wet

■ Made in the USA

52 BUILD YOUR OWN ICE RINK

Whether your family likes to practice hockey, figure skating, or curling, what they really need is a patch of ice to call their own. A small financial investment can yield big returns of family fun when you build your own backyard ice rink.

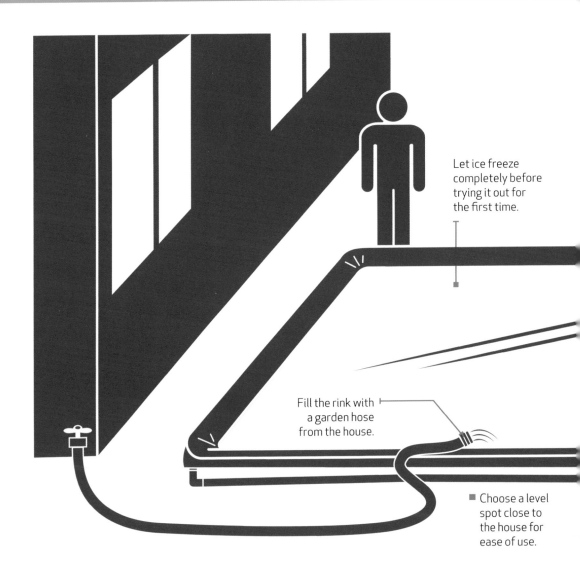

Let ice freeze completely before trying it out for the first time.

Fill the rink with a garden hose from the house.

■ Choose a level spot close to the house for ease of use.

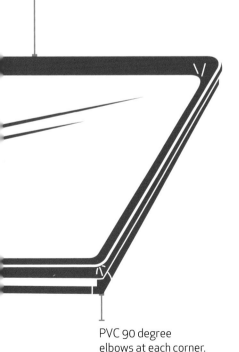

Plan the right number of PVC pieces for the "walls" of the rink and make sure you don't build it bigger than the size of your tarp.

PVC 90 degree elbows at each corner.

STEP 1 Scope out your yard for a piece of flat ground within reach of your garden hose. Use a carpenter's long level sitting atop a straight piece of lumber to see if the ground really is level—wishful thinking can make us see "level" areas almost anywhere. Use a tape measure to determine the actual dimensions of the area.

STEP 2 Assemble your supplies. Once you know the size of your rink, sketch it out on paper to determine your materials. For the rink's perimeter, use 4-inch (10-cm) schedule 20 PVC sewer pipe (it won't rot, like wood, and it's lightweight, easy to assemble, and quick to break down). You'll also need four "elbows" (the corner pieces) of the same pipe size. Finally, you'll need a 6-mm (or thicker) polyethylene plastic tarp or liner. This should be one solid piece. Don't try to splice it at home.

STEP 3 Assemble your rink. Slip the male pipe ends into the female ends, laying out your rink walls. If you purchased elbows that have one male and one female end, no extra fittings are needed, and the whole perimeter should slip together without a problem. Do not glue the joints! You'll want to break these walls down each spring and store the pieces so that your rink lasts for several years. When you've assembled the perimeter wall, spread out your liner. Make sure it drapes over the wall on every side.

STEP 4 Fill 'er up! With the rink frame finished, simply fill with water and let the freezing air do the rest. Don't overfill—just go halfway up to start—as too much water pressure will push the walls outward. Once filled, the water will naturally level itself, so the skating surface should be smooth and even. When you've enjoyed the rink enough that the ice has become rough, add more water and let it freeze again for a brand-new surface.

Now bring out some lawn chairs and hot drinks, strap on your skates, and enjoy the show!

EMERGENCY

NATURE'S WRATH CAN BE SEVERE,

especially when ice, snow, and wind combine to tear at our homes, knock out our power, and maroon us in a sea of white. Winter storms, freezing temperatures, medical concerns, mechanical issues, and other cold-weather emergencies can leave us vulnerable to a host of dangers. In this chapter, we'll brace for impact and devise alternatives when cut off from our regular sources of food, water, heat, and light— and we'll brainstorm action plans when faced with disaster scenarios. This can be a scary state of affairs, but don't panic. Humans have survived winter for millennia with just a few basic supplies, their ingenuity, and the will to live. You can survive, too.

53 DECIDE TO STAY OR GO

The weather forecast says a blizzard is on the way, and it's time to decide what to do in the time you have left before the storm. Do you make a mad dash to the grocery store for milk, bread, and toilet paper? Do you barricade yourself inside? Or do you get out of town? Every situation is different, so consider these factors to create a safe and practical plan.

UNDERSTAND THE FORECAST

Find out if there is real cause for alarm before you hunker down or flee. Listen to multiple meteorologists to get an idea of the conditions of the upcoming storm. Try to find out when the snow will start falling, how long it will last, and what they're estimating for snowfall totals, wind speeds, and low temperatures. Arm yourself with information before you get all "Chicken Little" on your family.

FIND A BETTER PLACE

Jetting off to the Caribbean may not be an option before the next blizzard, but you may find that neighboring regions won't be hit as hard. If it's practical and the roads are safe to travel, it might not be a bad idea to go visit your friends or relatives in gentler climates. Make sure you close down your home before leaving (see item 1).

DECIDE IF YOU'RE READY

Find out just how prepared you really are. Take stock of your food, water, backup lighting and heating methods, alternative power, and all other necessities before you make a decision to stay put. Riding out the storm while underprepared can be uncomfortable—or downright dangerous.

54 PREPARE FOR A BLIZZARD

Before you get cut off from the world by a giant wall of ice and snow, make sure you have everything you'd need to hunker down for a few days. I wasn't kidding about stocking up on milk, bread, and toilet paper—if the power goes out, the milk can still be drunk, the bread can make no-cook meals like sandwiches, and the toilet paper has dozens of applications. But that's not all you'll need, so stock these crucial items before the blizzard hits.

HEAT One of the most critical items is an emergency heating option. Grab a kerosene or propane heater designed for indoor use—they'll be clearly labeled on the packaging. Many also have added safety features.

FOOD If the power goes out, feed your troops with foods that don't require cooking.

RADIO Get a small weather radio with the NOAA weather bands and alert tones so you'll know if the storm takes a turn for the worse.

GAMES Stash a few activities like books, games, and other pastimes—you'll look like a hero when your family is going stir crazy.

MEDS & HYGIENE Refill any prescriptions and stock up on common over-the-counter meds. Ensure there are enough toiletries for everyone, and that the ladies of the house have a good supply of feminine hygiene products.

55 IDENTIFY DEAL BREAKERS

Some things you can live without. Other things are non-negotiable. If a severe winter storm is predicted for your area, take the time to assess all of your critical preparations. If you find something vital is ruined or missing, load up the family for an impromptu vacation and head someplace safer.

DEAL BREAKERS	
NO HEATING ALTERNATIVES	Almost all homes require electricity to provide their winter heating. Having no backup leaves your family in a cold and precarious position if the storm takes down the power lines.
NO WATER	For rural homes with a well, power loss means water loss. Unless you have a crafty system (like a gravity-fed spring water supply), your well water is hard to reach without the pump. If you don't have an extra supply of water, you might not want to try your luck against a blizzard.
NO POWER PRODUCTION	Winter storms can leave a remote home without power for days or even weeks. Consider investing in a generator with adequate fuel for several days, or consider bugging out before the first snowflakes hit the ground.

56 TAKE ON TOUGH JOBS

There's a pantry full of bottled water and canned goods. The family is dressed warmly and you're ready for the worst. Riding out a blizzard at home shouldn't rattle the household too much, assuming that the power and water stay on. There's only one thing left to do as the flakes start to fall: Set up your home for an easier "dig out."

STRATEGIZE SNOW REMOVAL Place your snow shovels (yes, you should have more than one) by your doors for easy access in case you need to dig yourself out. Keep gloves, boots, coats, and other gear near the door, and shovel often to keep up with the storm (see item 20).

PREPARE PETS AND LIVESTOCK Bring in your pets. Blizzards are as dangerous to most companion animals as they are to humans who might get caught outside. If you have livestock, shut them in their shelters and lay out extra food. You should also make a plan to get them water—even if the power fails and the snow gets deep.

TEST THE SNOW BLOWER If you are fortunate enough to own one of these snow-throwing wonders, ensure it is operational before you actually need it. Make sure it has plenty of fuel and oil, that the engine starts, and that the auger works.

HIRE A PRO If you don't want to shovel or plow your driveway by yourself, get on the books ahead of time to receive service from a professional.

57 HUNKER DOWN AND WAIT

As the storm dumps its snow and ice upon your region, the best thing you can do is stay home. Even a multi-day storm must come to an end sometime. But while you wait, here are a few chores and activities to keep you from feeling idle.

GET COOKING Prepare a fancy dinner for the family. Get them involved and make everything from scratch. By the time you've cooked, eaten, and cleaned up all the mess, you'll be ready for bed—or at least a nap.

RUN SOME WATER In a blizzard with high wind and deep cold, keep a few of your faucets dripping to keep the pipes from freezing and bursting. Keep a pitcher under each one and use the water around the house (no need to waste it!)

DO PROCRASTINATED WORK If you feel the need to accomplish something, tackle a dreaded chore. Start your taxes, do some bookkeeping, clean a room—do any project that satisfies your need for industry.

58 STAVE OFF BOREDOM

The term "cabin fever" was first coined in the 1800s, and neither you, nor your family and friends, should suffer from this preventable form of historical grouchiness. If you forgot to buy some new novels before the storm hit, use these tried and true time-killers.

BINGE-WATCH A TV SHOW A couple of long-running dramas with snack and bathroom breaks in between can take up a whole day. To mix it up a little, watch some as a family and watch others separately (depending on age-appropriateness). Hopefully you remembered hot cocoa and popcorn on your pre-storm shopping trip.

DO SOME CHORES Go split some wood or do some other tiring tasks. And hey, you could also start shoveling.

MAKE SOME ART Your snow day art projects are only limited by your imagination. Paint, color, sculpt, carve, build, or even destroy; as long as it looks interesting at the end, you can call it art.

HIBERNATE Sometimes the bears and the groundhogs have the right idea: Take a nap or hit the hay early. Wake me when it's over.

PLAY DURING THE STORM Barring dangerous conditions, it could be fun to get out into the snow for a few minutes. Don't wander off and get lost in a whiteout, but try out your new snowshoes in the yard or start on that Olympic-sized snowman.

BRING OUT A GAME I used to think they were called "bored games" because you only played them when you were ... well, you get the idea. A long board game can fill the hours—or maybe poker is more your speed. Either way, have the supplies on hand to play a few rounds.

59 PERSEVERE SANS POWER

You're snowbound and the power just went out. It's time to put your plans into action. I always find it helpful to plan for (and expect) the worst, but hope for the best—then, when things aren't completely horrible, you'll be pleasantly surprised. Here are the first things to do when the power goes down.

- Turn on some safe alternative lighting. Be wary of candles if you have clumsy or rambunctious kids or pets (or adults). Use battery-powered lighting.

- Start conserving mobile power. You're likely to be using your phone or tablet to access the world outside, so use it wisely. Rather than wasting battery power to Instagram pictures of your family in awful sweaters, update Facebook so people know you're safe, but snowed in without power.

- Begin using heat conservation and alternative heating methods. It's easier to keep the existing warmth in than it is to heat a cold house.

- Think about dinner. An army moves on its stomach, and so does a family. Set up your alternative cooking methods and start working on your next meal.

60 SAVE SOME FOOD

Just because the power is out doesn't mean that all of the foods in your fridge are a lost cause. Some common fridge items don't have to be refrigerated, and may last a long time at room temperature.

BUTTER This delicious dairy product can last several days at room temperature, but try to use it quickly.

POTATOES Spuds are happy in dark, moist places, but this doesn't have to be in the refrigerator. Keep them in a bin in a cabinet until they begin to sprout.

ONIONS These root veggies do well in an airy dark spot, but keep them away from your potatoes—they often spoil them faster.

CONDIMENTS Spreads like mustard, hot sauce, and ketchup are salty and acidic enough to last a while. Open, they will keep for a month at room temperature.

SOY SAUCE Dark and seductively saline, soy sauce has a high enough salt content to last indefinitely—even without any refrigeration.

GARLIC This pungent bulb likes air circulation, and there's no need to keep it in the fridge. Garlic should keep for three to five months in a cool, dry, dark place.

61 STEP TOWARD FOOD SAFETY

So how long does a thawing package of hot dogs last when your home's interior temperature is cold, but variable? Since you never know how long a power outage will last, assume that you'll be without power for at least a few days, and follow these steps to keep your household well-fed with safe foods.

STEP 1 Don't open the fridge or freezer without a good reason. The longer the doors stay shut, the longer the temperature will be stable. An unopened refrigerator will keep food cold for about four hours, and a packed freezer will hold its temperature for about two days (24 hours if it's only half-stocked).

STEP 2 Plan your meals based on what you know to be in the freezer and fridge, such as making a big pot of soup to incorporate lots of random fresh ingredients. When you do have to open the freezer or fridge to pull something out, place a thermometer in each to help you track the temperature.

STEP 3 If the power has been off for more than four hours, it's now time to move to Plan B: placing refrigerated food in coolers with snow or ice. Keep these coolers in a cold garage or nearby shed for easy access and protection from animals. Dispose of any perishable meats, poultry, seafood, raw eggs, or leftover foods that have been above 40° F (4° C) for two hours or more.

STEP 4 Once the refrigerated food has been eaten (or thrown away if questionable), start working your way through the frozen food. Never taste foods to determine its safety—toss anything with an unusual odor, color, or texture, as well as anything that feels warm. If in doubt, throw it out.

62

TURN YOUR FRIDGE INTO AN ICEBOX

With the power out, bring back old-school refrigeration techniques by turning your refrigerator (already an insulated box) into an icebox. Freeze plastic bags or plastic tubs of water during the blizzard—you can leave them outside, frozen solid, until needed. If the power fails, place these small ice blocks around your food in the refrigerator and freezer to help keep food cold. Safe temperatures are 40° F (4° C) or lower in the refrigerator and 0° F (-18° C) or lower in the freezer.

63 COOK WITHOUT UTILITIES

Dinner doesn't have to be a disaster when you're assembling meals during a winter emergency. Even though your success depends on many factors (the food on hand, how it was stored, when it will expire, and what cooking methods are available), you can still use these alternative methods to prepare great food while the utilities are down.

	TIPS	WHAT TO MAKE
GAS GRILL	Boiling water can lead to better things, including soup, oatmeal, and coffee. Use the BBQ, but only outdoors. Grills aren't safe for indoor or garage use.	Boil water, bake a frozen pizza, or bundle up for a cold-weather BBQ.
SOLAR OVEN	A handy tool for slow-cooking food on a cold but sunny day.	Slow-cooker roasts, stews, and soups.
CAMPFIRE	Build it in the backyard and you'll have a timeless go-to.	Eat like our ancestors, over an open flame. If all else fails, make s'mores!
CAMP OR ALCOHOL STOVES	Portability makes these very handy for on-the-go and kitchen-less cooking.	Fry up some eggs, sear some burgers, or prepare anything else you'd eat on a camping trip.
AUTO ENGINE	Wrap your food in foil and stick it on the vehicle engine to cook in a pinch.	Toast bread and heat leftovers—just watch the gas gauge.

64 LEARN HEARTH COOKING

For centuries, people have cooked in their home fireplaces. The hearth provided heat, light, and several modes of cooking. These historical techniques can still work today, as long as you have the right equipment.

TRY A DUTCH OVEN The same Dutch ovens used for campfire cooking can be used in a fireplace. Build up a bed of coals, then nestle the covered pot of food in the embers and use a fireplace shovel to place some coals on the lid. Replace the coals on top of the Dutch oven as they burn down to ash. Bake or broil foods for lengths of time comparable to oven baking.

USE SPITS AND KABOBS Cooking meat on spits, skewers, and hooks was very popular in medieval times. There was even a breed of tiny dog that was used to turn hearth spits by running in wheel-shaped cages. You can avoid the need for a rotisserie motor or hamster wheel by turning the

rods yourself (every 5 to 10 minutes). Use metal rods to impale food and suspend them with wire over the flames of your fire.

USE GOOD WOOD Practice caution when selecting the wood you burn for cooking. Don't use pressure-treated lumber, painted wood, and other potentially hazardous materials, as their smoke can be toxic.

65

BUILD A TUNA CAN STOVE

If you have a few bricks, an empty tuna can, and rubbing alcohol, you can build a small stove to heat water or food. All you need is a stable, fireproof spot to set up—and keep a fire extinguisher handy, just in case.

STEP 1 On a fireproof surface, use several bricks for a hearth.

STEP 2 Place the empty tuna can on the hearth and fill it halfway with rubbing alcohol. Be careful to avoid spills and overfilling.

STEP 3 Light the alcohol in the can with a stick match. Since burning alcohol can be very difficult to see, use caution to avoid burning your fingers.

STEP 4 Place your pot or pan on the raised bricks, over the stove. If one pour of alcohol isn't enough to complete your

cooking, wait until the can has burned out completely before adding more alcohol. Pouring alcohol into a burning stove can be very dangerous.

66

LIGHT UP THE DARK

As humans don't have much in the way of natural night vision, the darkness can be disconcerting; good thing there are so many ways to light up your home.

FLASHLIGHTS The most common backup lighting, flashlights come in a wide array of styles and with a variety of features. Look for LED bulbs to make your lights last longer. And don't forget the extra batteries.

LIGHT STICKS Light sticks are a nice backup, too. The common 8-hour green chem light is a good choice. You can find various colors; white is the closest match to the illumination of a flashlight. In the cold, the light won't glow as brightly, but will last longer. For more light, drop the stick in boiling water for a minute or two—it will glow more brightly, but it will have lost about half of its life span.

CANDLES Make sure your candles are located in a fire-resistant spot (not sitting under the drapes), and are sturdy. If the wicks burn out before the wax is consumed, use a hot metal nail to burrow a hole and insert a piece of cotton twine for a new wick.

IMPROVISED LAMPS With the proper wick, you can turn almost any oil into an oil lamp. All you need is a fireproof container, a fuel source, and a wick. Grab a jar or can, or mold a tinfoil tray, and insert a wick (cotton balls are great, but any natural plant fiber will work). Fill your container with an inch (2.5 cm) of whatever oil you're using as fuel. You can use olive oil, paraffin lamp oil, or even used cooking oil. Light the wick with an open flame, such as a lighter or a match.

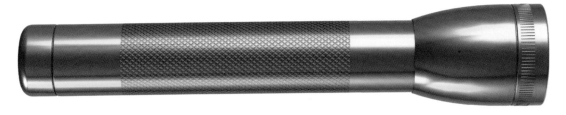

67

HANDLE SAFE HEATING

Don't replace one danger with another by swapping hypothermia for a house fire. Rely on these safety tips to keep a bad situation from getting worse.

PICK A ROOM Don't try to heat the whole house. Use only one small room with a low ceiling as your main living area during the power outage. Don't try to make every room warm again. It's a waste of time and resources.

VENTILATE Don't use combustion without ventilation—you're just begging for carbon monoxide poisoning if you use a propane heater, a grill, or a gas stove as a heat source. Even a kerosene heater needs fresh air.

MODERATE Candles are a problematic heat source, often causing home fires in already troubling emergencies. If you're using enough candles to warm a room, you have a serious fire hazard on your hands. Limit their use, and make sure you have a working smoke alarm with a carbon monoxide detector.

68 USE BRICKS AND STONES

While you can't heat a room with hand-warmer packs, you can certainly heat yourself by keeping a few in your pockets. Building on that concept of portable radiant heat, you can also turn rocks and bricks into space heaters.

STEP 1 Safety first! You'll need to set up a heatproof platform—a 2-foot (0.6-m) square of bricks lying on the floor works fine. Then get some rocks or bricks from a dry location.

STEP 2 Fire up the grill, or build a fire outside, and throw in the rocks (or bricks) for about 45 minutes. Then scoop them out with a shovel and remove all the coals and sparks.

STEP 3 Drop your hot bricks or rocks into a stainless steel pot. The heat can damage other types of pots, or release toxic vapors (as with galvanized buckets). Stick with the steel pot.

STEP 4 Carefully bring the hot rocks or bricks inside and set the pot of hot stuff on your fireproof, heatproof platform. Enjoy the radiant heat from your DIY space heater, and repeat as needed every few hours.

69 HEAT WITH THE SUN

A grid-down, cold-weather emergency can leave the home dangerously cold. Death from hypothermia is a real threat, but there is an easy and safe way to gain heat by managing the sun that's shining into your dwelling. Yes, a home heating solar array on your roof would be ideal, but you can get warm using the assets that you already have.

Take advantage of passive solar heat during daylight hours by staying in rooms with south-facing windows. Lay out dark-colored blankets to absorb the heat. The more sun pouring through the windows and the more dark colors you place in the light, the more heat you will collect. Then use thick drapes or improvised insulation to block the chill coming off the windows after sundown.

10 EMERGENCY USES FOR CANS

Aluminum beverage cans and steel food cans may be garbage in your daily life. But it's fair to say that one man's trash truly is another man's treasure—particularly in an emergency situation. Here are ten survival uses for the humble yet handy empty metal can.

BOILING VESSEL Whether your metal can is aluminum or steel, it can be used as a great boiling vessel. Fill it with questionable water and set it in the ashes to boil.

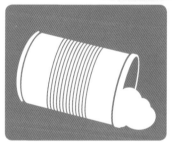

DIGGING TOOL Sturdy cans are great for digging, particularly in soft or sandy soils. Use the can to dig fire pits, cat holes, and anything else you need in and around camp.

SIGNAL ALARM Attach a can full of stones (or several cans together) to thread or fishing line, perch it on the edge of your camp, and run the line around camp as a tripwire.

STOVE Pierce holes for air intake around the bottom of a large can, and cut a few square teeth into the top lip for pot stand legs. Wear your gloves!

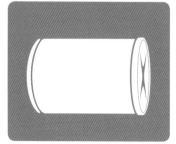

TRAP Make a foot trap by plunging your knife twice into the end, creating an X. Push the points inward for a small opening, and wire it to a stake in the ground.

MIRROR Depending on your can and your polishing skills, you may be able to buff a section of the can to create a reflective surface. Use it as an improvised signal mirror.

FARADAY CAGE Threat of EMPs got you down? Wrap up your electronics in insulating materials, and place them in a large can to simulate a Faraday cage. There are no guarantees, but who knows? It might help.

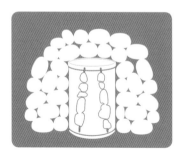

LOW-TECH OVEN Large cans, make excellent ovens when covered with hot coals. Impale your meat or veggies on a stake, cover with the can, and bury in hot coals.

CHAR CLOTH CONTAINER Cut the top off an aluminum can and fill the can with cattail fluff, cotton cloth, linen, or bark fiber. Fold closed and place in a fire for 5 minutes.

FIRE CARRIER Attach a loop of wire to a metal can to make a handle. Fill with tinder (fungus, rotten wood, bark). Drop in some hot hardwood coals and carry your fire.

71 WALK IN A WHITEOUT

A whiteout is an extreme weather condition in which heavy windblown or falling snow reduces visibility almost to zero; going out in it could send you way off course. Don't travel in this weather if you can avoid it, but if you must wander through a whiteout, here's how.

GEAR UP It's a very dangerous course of action to walk through the blinding snow. There had better be a good reason for it, because generally speaking, you should be staying put. However, if an emergency calls for foot travel in a whiteout, make sure to dress the part. Wear appropriate outerwear, including a parka, snow pants, snow boots, mittens, a face mask, and goggles.

BLAZE A TRAIL Since visibility is the biggest issue in these conditions, make use of markers to find your way. Stick dark-colored poles in the snow every few yards (or meters) to create a visible path through the snow.

GET SOME HELP Use a compass or GPS to stay on track during a whiteout. For even more security on short trips that are often repeated (like the trek from cabin to outhouse and back again), set up a long rope line before the storm to use as a handrail.

WALK THE TRAIL As a last-ditch effort to find your way back through a whiteout, look or feel for the tracks you made in the snow earlier.

72 DRIVE THROUGH A WHITEOUT

Step one for driving through a whiteout is to rethink driving through a whiteout. Step two? Don't drive through a whiteout. But if there is some pressing need that cannot wait, then you may have to embark on a white-knuckled ride through the white stuff. Day or night, visibility and traction are the two biggest problems when driving in these conditions. Use these tricks to make this trek possible.

TAKE IT EASY Avoid sudden moves in acceleration, braking, and steering. Jerking the wheel or stomping on the gas or brake can leave you slipping and sliding all over the road. Focus on smooth maneuvers.

USE CHAINS Whiteout conditions are often accompanied by snow accumulations on the road surface. Be ready to install pre-fitted tire chains to your tires.

FLASH YOUR HAZARDS You can help the other crazy drivers to see you by using your hazard flashers during the entire trip.

CHECK YOUR FLUIDS Make sure you have a full reservoir of low-temperature washer fluid in the vehicle, to help keep your windshield clean.

PULL OVER If conditions worsen and you can't see, pull over in a safe place and keep your flashers on to stay visible. Be prepared to enter a snowbound vehicle scenario.

GO SLOW Forget about speed limits—they're for dry, clear conditions. Drive slowly and watch your speedometer. It's easy to speed up without realizing it in your haste to be done with the dangerous trip.

73 SPOT HYPOTHERMIA

Hypothermia is a medical condition that occurs when a person's core temperature drops below 95° F (35° C). This dangerous condition can be caused by exposure to water, wind, very cold air, or a combination of these elements. Be alert to these signs in yourself and others in order to catch hypothermia while it is still treatable.

MILD

Shivering • Confusion • Slurred speech • Numbness or tingling in the skin • Sluggish muscles (a good indicator of a cold body before shivering begins)

MODERATE

Violent shivering • Clumsiness • Lack of coordination • Pale skin • Blue-colored lips, ears, fingers, and toes

SEVERE

Difficulty speaking • Trouble walking • Amnesia • Extreme tiredness • Irrational behavior (such as removing clothing or burrowing into snow, sand, or other material)

74 FIGHT BACK AGAINST THE COLD

Rewarming is the main method of treatment for hypothermia victims. Use one of these methods (or a combination of techniques) based on the severity of the cold exposure.

PASSIVE EXTERNAL REWARMING This type of rewarming involves the use of the body's own heat-generating ability. Get the victim out of his wet clothes and into some properly insulated dry clothing and a warm environment. Give a little high calorie food and warm sips of a hot beverage if the hypothermia is mild.

ACTIVE EXTERNAL REWARMING Apply warming devices externally, such as a hot water bottle in both armpits. Never use hot baths to treat a hypothermic person, as it can cause a heart attack.

ACTIVE CORE REWARMING Core rewarming should only be administered by a professional, as it involves the use of intravenous warmed fluids, irrigation of body cavities with warmed fluids, use of warm humidified inhaled air, or use of extracorporeal rewarming such as a heart-lung machine. These techniques are impractical, impossible, or dangerous to attempt in the field. If you are forced to treat this level of hypothermia, be aware that victims often go into shock as they rewarm.

75 DON'T BELIEVE THE HYPE

The cold is one of humanity's oldest adversaries, and over the millennia we have had plenty of time to create myths and misinformation about the treatment of hypothermia. Unfortunately, many of these false remedies have spread far and wide enough to become gospel. It's important to educate yourself on the difference between fact and fiction, especially when it comes to necessary medical treatments in a survival situation.

MYTH	REALITY
A SIP OF LIQUOR WILL CURE HYPOTHERMIA	While strong drink (namely liquor) may have a place in some survival scenarios, it is the last beverage you should chug if you are in the grip of cold-weather exposure. Alcohol can move more blood to the skin and dull the pain of the cold, making you feel warmer. But as this happens, your body's core will chill faster, which only harms you further. Instead, take small sips of a warm drink like hot tea or hot cocoa.
WALK IT OFF	Exercise has been documented as saving lives in near-hypothermic cases, but the loss of critical body heat can result in a loss of dexterity, poor mental state, a loss of consciousness, and clumsiness. Trying to jog or do any vigorous exercise will definitely tire the victim out, and he could fall, adding broken bones to the situation. Skip the jumping jacks and get him into dry clothing, a warm shelter, or the proximity of a roaring fire. Don't try to walk off this injury.
IT'S OK TO SLEEP WHILE HYPOTHERMIC	A few minutes in cold water, or a few hours in the cold wind, can send someone's body deep into hypothermia. After the shivering, confusion, slurred speech, numbness, and clumsiness have manifested, a cold-exposure victim will also get very tired. This weariness is a very serious warning sign. Hypothermia victims often go to sleep just before dying. Keep her awake at all costs as you warm her up.
A HOT BATH, HOT TUB, OR SAUNA WILL CURE HYPOTHERMIA	Rewarming someone is the main method of cold-exposure treatment, both in the field and in the hospital. But dropping somebody in the Jacuzzi will be excruciatingly painful, and it can even cause a heart attack. Active external rewarming can be done on the patient by applying warm items externally, and skin-on-skin rewarming is also safe and gentle (although potentially awkward). Never use hot baths, steam rooms, or any other high heat to treat a hypothermic person.
DON'T FEED A HYPOTHERMIC PERSON	Normal shock treatment and hypothermia treatment are different, yet often confused with one another. You don't want to feed someone who may be going into shock because he could vomit and choke while unconscious. In mild to moderate hypothermia cases, however, high-calorie foods can be given in small, repeated doses to create metabolic heat. Get him out of his wet clothes, get him into some insulated dry clothing, and provide high-calorie food and sips of a hot beverage.

76 FACTOR IN FROSTBITE

Frostbite occurs when ice forms in your skin and tissues. Your skin will often go numb right before frostbite. Later (when the tissues thaw out), there's an intense burning pain. Frostbite can be a common injury during the winter months, especially in northern regions, at high altitude, and under windy conditions. Watch for these signs in yourself and others to prevent frostbite, and catch it while it is still treatable in the field.

PREVENT THE PROBLEM The best preventative measure you can take is to recognize the conditions that cause frostbite and to keep all skin warmly covered. Temperatures in the 20° F (-7° C) range can lead to frostbite, if strong winds are present or if there has been enough exposure time. Temperatures near or below 0° F (-18° C), with any wind, are swift to produce frostbite on exposed skin and extremities like fingers, toes, ears, and noses. Wind speeds

over 20 mph (32 kph) at temperatures below 0° F (-18° C) are very likely to create frostbite in hours or even minutes.

FACE THE FACTS Superficial frostbite commonly occurs in patches on exposed areas of the face, but it can also occur on the hands, ears, fingers, and toes. These patches of skin may look dull in color, waxy, and pale, and feel firm to the touch. The underlying tissue will still feel soft, and the victim may feel pain in these areas.

DON'T GO TOO FAR Deep frostbite happens when deeper tissues and more extensive tissue become frozen. The skin will be pale and firm, and the underlying tissues will feel solid. Feet, legs, hands, and arms may be lost due to this severe level of frostbite. Tissues with deep frostbite will generally feel numb, and joint movement will feel restricted.

77 BITE BACK

The treatment of frostbite is usually a painful process that involves rewarming the skin and tissues. This can be done in the field or in a hospital, but should only be attempted if there is no danger of refreezing. Here's how to treat frostbite:

STEP 1 Identify the type of frostbite. Superficial frostbite occurs in patches, which may look dull in color and waxy, while deep frostbite causes the skin to turn pale and firm (see item 76, left).

STEP 2 Rewarm the skin and tissues—unless there is a danger of refreezing. In cases of superficial frostbite, place a warm body part against the frostbitten tissue. Deep frostbite requires hot water at stable temperatures around 105° F (40.5° C). Treat with pain medication as you begin rewarming. Ibuprofen is a good choice for the pain, and it should be taken before the pain becomes too bad. Do not rub frostbitten areas, as more pain and damage will result.

STEP 3 Protect that tissue from refreezing at all costs. Make sure to monitor the victim for signs of hypothermia and shock, as well.

78 CONTINUE YOUR CARE

Deep frostbite is usually accompanied by incredible pain and a high chance of infection. The affected tissue can still be in danger even months after the injury occurred. Frostbite kills healthy cells, leaving the area full of dead tissue, which often turns black and must be surgically removed. Otherwise, it will become a source of infection for the surrounding surviving tissue. Keep up a regimen of daily care for several weeks. Most skin grafting and amputations occur three or four weeks after the injury.

Avoid smoking during the healing process, as nicotine is a vasoconstrictor, slowing blood flow and healing. Eat a high-calorie, high-protein diet to fuel the body for the best chance of successful self-repair.

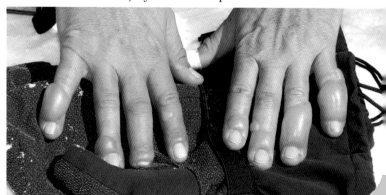

79 KEEP YOUR TOES TOASTY

The value of a great pair of boots can never be overstated. If a person's feet become frostbitten or injured in an emergency, their chances for survival take a nosedive. This brings me to my favorite pair of winter hiking boots. While some others are better suited for sub-zero living, they are harder to hike in and even harder to wear while doing heavy work.

COOL TOOLS
BOOTS

After purchasing several pairs of allegedly waterproof boots over the last few years (sadly, they all leaked), and teaching survival classes in cold wet environs, I was thrilled to finally find a pair of boots that lived up to their claims. Rocky's S2V Substratum boots have been touted as the survival boot that won't quit, and with good reason.

550 cord laces have a variety of survival uses

Crampon- and snowshoe-compatible

The waterproof and insulated uppers protect your feet from cold, wet conditions

Secret compartment in the heel, with fire-starting supplies included

80 ENJOY THE FEATURES

The Substratum boots may look a little space-age at first glance, but they're chock-full of classic features to protect your feet—along with the rest of you.

GRAB SOME CORD AND FIRE

550 paracord bootlaces are a nice touch, but they're not even the best survival concept built into the boot design. These boots come with a compact, one-hand-operated fire starter (Sparkie) and Wetfire cubes from Ultimate Survival Technologies, with a comfortable secret storage space in each boot to make sure you never get caught without fire-making materials. The insoles of either boot can be pulled free and a small foam spacer removed to create a caddy in the heel of each boot for the spark rod, fire cubes, and other survival kit items that you may want to stuff in there. This could be a great little hiding spot for cash, a spare set of keys, or whatever you might need while traveling.

HOLD BACK THE COLD

To protect you from the elements, the upper is waterproof Nubuck leather and ripstop nylon. A fully gusseted tongue and high top helps to keep out rocks, snow, and water. The Hydro IQ (waterproof/air circulation) technology of the boots uses a moisture-wicking lining to keep the interior dry, and includes a molded antimicrobial insole. The insole is bright pink in color, so you could even use it to signal for help. The bottom of the boots are crampon and snowshoe compatible, which allows you to wear them throughout the entire winter. As a bonus, the wave underlay proves excellent traction. Together, the boots weigh 4.25 pounds (1.92 kg). Below is a summary of the specs.

- Crampon and snowshoe compatible

- Molded foam padded with high-abrasion Lycra and antimicrobial space mesh

- Bright pink, tri-density, molded antimicrobial insole

- Open-cell foam forefoot with polyurethane top layer

- Polyurethane-enhanced toe wrap and extended back guard

- Polyurethane, direct attached for superior longevity and a permanent outsole bond

- Proprietary wave underlay texture for element traction and shedding

- Moisture-wicking lining

- Fully gusseted tongue for performance comfort

- UST essentials located within outsole: firesparker and wetcubes (x2)

- 550 military-grade paracord bootlaces

81 PREP FOR CAR TROUBLES

It's almost funny (almost!) how the car always breaks down in awful weather. Here are some of things that might go wrong—and how to deal.

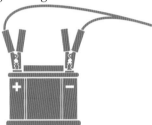

DEAL WITH THE DEAD The cold is notorious for sucking the life from our poor batteries. If your engine won't turn over or your starter makes a rapid clicking sound, you likely need a jumpstart. Carefully connect the red jumper cable clamps to the positive posts of the good and bad batteries. Connect one black clamp to the black post (negative) of the good battery. Connect the other black clamp to a piece of grounded metal on the dead car. Start the good car, rev the engine for 30 seconds, and then try to start the dead car. If it won't start, wait a few minutes and try again. If several attempts don't work, you'll need to go buy a new battery (or something else was wrong).

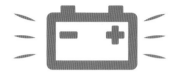

WATCH YOUR ALTERNATOR A faulty alternator is a common source of cold-climate mechanical problems and can kill a battery quick. The alternator provides power to your car's battery and other electrical components such as the headlights and wipers. If you notice a flickering battery warning light, dim headlights or dashboard lights, or slower windshield wipers, it may be time to have your alternator replaced before it leaves you stranded.

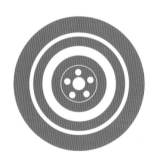

CARRY A SPARE Shockingly, many car manufacturers are cutting fiscal corners by eliminating spare tires as standard equipment. If you don't have a spare, pick one up at a tire dealer. Potholes and rough roads can destroy perfectly good tires. And while you're checking the trunk, make sure you have a tire iron and functional jack.

COOL IT DOWN A great irony of winter driving is that your vehicle can still overheat, often due to leaky hoses and damaged radiators. Regularly top off your coolant and never add plain water, which will freeze. If you get stuck with a dry coolant reservoir, detach your wiper fluid line from the sprayer nozzle and run it into your coolant reservoir, then hit the button for the windshield fluid to pump a stream of alcohol and cleaning fluid into the reservoir. It's not healthy for your radiator, but it will work in a pinch. Once back in the loving arms of civilization, treat your vehicle to a full radiator flush and refill—and make sure the mechanics find the leak.

82 TAKE STEPS BEFORE THE STORM

You only have yourself to blame when preventable problems come into play. Make sure you take care of your vehicle while you can.

REPLACE BATTERIES Your vehicle's battery has one of the toughest winter jobs. Low temps affect the performance of any battery, but older ones are especially vulnerable. Have your battery tested in the fall to find out if it needs to be replaced. Also be sure to check the battery cables and terminals, make sure the connections are tight, and brush away any corrosion.

CHOOSE LOW-TEMP FLUID Mid-drive is not the time to realize that your washer fluid has frozen into a sheet of ice on the windshield. Replace it with the low-temp variety.

CHECK YOUR BELTS Inspect the vehicle's drive belts for cracks or fraying. Look at the underside, where most wear occurs. The smooth surface won't show their true condition.

INSPECT YOUR HOSES Check your cooling system hoses for leaks, cracks, or loose clamps. Replace if needed.

WATCH YOUR WIPERS Replace streaky wiper blades and consider installing a set that wraps the blade in a rubber boot to prevent ice buildup.

DON'T GET TIRED Change out your balding, dangerous tires with snow tires. Replace any tire with less than $3/32$ inches ($1/4$ cm) of tread depth. Spring for an alignment to prevent uneven wear.

FEEL THE PRESSURE Check your tire pressure often, and add air as needed.

PREVENT A BRAKE FAILURE Get your brakes inspected by a certified technician. You're going to need them.

83 STAY ALIVE IN YOUR RIDE

So you managed to start your vehicle and drive out onto the roads. But the snow's a recipe for disaster, and when you hit a snowbank and get stuck, you're in real trouble. Hopefully you planned ahead, stocked your car, and got ready for the tasks ahead.

STEP 1 Call for help. Most folks have a mobile phone, so you should take the extra step and keep a car charger in your vehicle. The plug-in kind won't work if the vehicle has a dead battery, so self-contained recharging systems are a safer bet. Solar chargers, battery pack chargers, and even hand-crank devices can help juice it.

STEP 2 If no help is coming, bundle up for warmth and try to dig the vehicle out. Make sure the vehicle is stocked with warm clothing and outerwear, as well as a shovel of some kind.

STEP 3 If the dig out fails, seek shelter in the car. High-energy food, water, and sleeping bags should be standard equipment for cold-weather travel. Add a small bucket with a tight-fitting lid and some hygiene products just in case. Run the engine for warmth occasionally, but only if you can keep the exhaust pipe clear. Vehicle exhaust can back up into the cabin when the exhaust pipe is buried in snow, mud, or water, and this will lead to carbon monoxide poisoning.

STEP 4 Create a signal for help outside the vehicle that can be spotted by passersby. Tie something colorful to the antenna and clear the snow off the roof so you can be seen from the ground and air. Use reflectors hanging on sticks around the vehicle. And never wander off to look for help. People who stay with their car generally make it, and those who don't are often lost.

84 LIGHT UP YOUR NIGHT

Emergency lighting can be a real lifesaver, especially if it helps someone spot your snowbound vehicle after dark.

BRING A FLASHLIGHT Obvious solutions to your lack of lighting, flashlights and headlamps can provide light and signal for help. Make sure you have spare batteries.

LIGHT A CANDLE Though it's a bit of a fire hazard, you can light a small candle (like a tea light) and place it on the vehicle's dashboard for light and a tiny bit of warmth. Don't light multiple candles, as they consume oxygen and a snowbound car lacks the airflow of an unburied vehicle. Health problems like hypoxia arise when you stay in a low-oxygen environment for an extended time. Signs and symptoms of this include tiredness, nausea, headache, and shortness of breath.

CRACK A GLOWSTICK OR LIGHT STICK This chemically-generated lighting can last a long time with none of the hazards of candles. The only drawback is that you cannot turn the activated sticks off and save them for later. These are one-hit wonders.

85 GENERATE EMERGENCY HEAT

While your derelict vehicle can keep you out of the wind and precipitation, all that metal will make it feel more like an icebox than a proper shelter. When the sun sets and the temperatures drop, use these techniques to stay warm (or warmer than you would have been) inside that cold steel box.

- Heat up stones in a fire outside the vehicle, then set them on the bare metal floorboard. To make body heaters rather than space heaters, warm the rocks slightly, wrap them in cloth, and hold them inside your clothing.

- Activate hand-warmer or foot-warmer packs and place them in your clothing. In a pinch, you could also use the ration heater from an MRE, but be aware that it makes a lot of steam. This could dampen your clothing and make you feel colder after the heater pack has burned out.

- If you can create some hot water, place it in a melt-proof bottle and wrap it in cloth or insert it into a sock. Stuff this old-fashioned hot water bottle into your clothes or sleeping bag for several hours of blessed warmth.

86 10 EMERGENCY USES FOR FOIL

Aluminum foil isn't just a convenient wrap for baked potatoes or a helmet to block alien mind probes—it's also pretty handy in a (real) emergency situation. Keep an extra roll in your kitchen or place a carefully folded length of foil in your bug-out bag, survival kit, and emergency gear stockpile. Here are ten of the many uses for this valuable commodity.

COOKING Whip up some roasted squirrel and wild herbs in a foil pouch for an appetizing emergency meal. You can even reuse the foil multiple times.

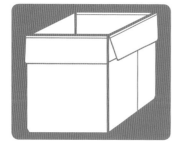

WATER BOILING Practice a little origami with paper to learn how to fold a square pot out of flat material. Once you've got the idea, fold your foil into a square or rectangular pot to boil water.

MIRROR A shiny piece of foil can provide a slightly reflective surface, usable as an improvised signal mirror.

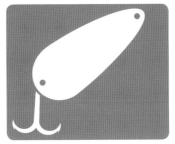

FISHING LURE Use foil wrapped around a bare fishhook to replicate the shape of a small fish or spoon. Secure it tightly and cast it out.

SOLAR OVEN Line a box with foil, place a dark pot in a clear oven bag, and set inside. Aim the open side of the box at the sun and slow-cook your feast.

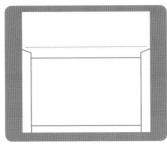

CONTAINER Fold the foil into an envelope or packet to act as a container for small items, or use it as a protective layer for larger items.

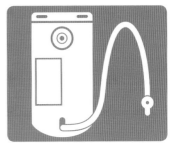

REPAIRS Something sticky (glue, pine sap) plus a foil strip can act as a temporary patch for pierced hydration bladders and cracked water bottles.

DRESSING POUCH Put clean cloth strips in a tightly folded foil packet and bake at a low temperature to create semi-sterile gauze for wounds.

SIGNAL STRIPS Tear off foil strips and dangle them on branches to make eye-catching, reflective flags. These can mark a path or signal for help.

LONG MATCH Fill some foil with shredded cedar or juniper bark, add a coal, and roll it up like a cigar. Leave one end open and transport your fire.

87 UNDERSTAND WIND CHILL

You've heard the term a million times, but what does it really mean? The weather forecast calls for a 20° F (-7° C) night, but the wind chill will be below zero (-18° C). To people from warmer climates, the math seems a little murky and the effect illogical—until they've experienced the shock of a cold blast of wind. Within seconds after exposure, skin can go from chilly yet comfortable to burning and stinging. Even though the temperature of skin and objects cannot drop below the ambient air temperature, no matter how great the wind speed, things can feel much colder than they really are as the icy

		TEMPERATURE (°F)							
CALM	40	35	30	25	20	15	10	5
5	36	31	25	19	13	7	1	-5
10	34	27	21	15	9	3	-4	-10
15	32	25	19	13	6	0	-7	-13
20	30	24	17	11	4	-2	-9	-15
25	29	23	16	9	3	-4	-11	-17
30	28	22	15	8	1	-5	-12	-19
35	28	21	14	7	0	-7	-14	-21
40	27	20	13	6	-1	-8	-15	-22
45	26	19	12	5	-2	-9	-16	-23
50	26	19	12	4	-3	-10	-17	-24
55	25	18	11	4	-3	-11	-18	-25
60	25	17	10	3	-4	-11	-19	-26

WIND (MPH)

wind continuously strips heat away. To worsen outdoor situations, if the ambient air temperature is below freezing, a significant wind chill factor can speed up the onset of frostbite and hypothermia. Use this chart to understand just how hazardous a cold wind can become.

FROSTBITE TIMES

30 minutes	10 minutes	5 minutes

0	-5	-10	-15	-20	-25	-30	-35	-40	-45
-11	-16	-22	-28	-34	-40	-46	-52	-57	-63
-16	-22	-28	-35	-41	-47	-53	-59	-66	-72
-19	-26	-32	-39	-45	-51	-58	-64	-71	-77
-22	-29	-35	-42	-48	-55	-61	-68	-74	-81
-24	-31	-37	-44	-51	-58	-64	-71	-78	-84
-26	-33	-39	-46	-53	-60	-67	-73	-80	-87
-27	-34	-41	-48	-55	-62	-69	-76	-82	-89
-29	-36	-43	-50	-57	-64	-71	-78	-84	-91
-30	-37	-44	-51	-58	-65	-72	-79	-86	-93
-31	-38	-45	-52	-60	-67	-74	-81	-88	-95
-32	-39	-46	-54	-61	-68	-75	-82	-89	-97
-33	-40	-48	-55	-62	-69	-76	-84	-91	-98

88

EAT FROM YOUR PACK

The MRE (Meal Ready to Eat) is a common military food ration—and if you ask any soldier who's eaten a few too many early prototypes, you'll hear some colorful interpretations (Meals Rarely Edible, among others). Since their development and wide distribution through the U.S. Armed Forces, MREs have caught on as a high-calorie, long-lasting food resource, often favored by preppers and emergency management folks. And they're really not bad at all, these days.

ENJOY YOUR ENTRÉE The entrée is the linchpin of the whole MRE. There are usually 12 MREs in a case, and many cases only have one or two menu repeats. Since 1993, a number of vegetarian, kosher, and halal meals have entered the mix.

HEAT THINGS UP The Flameless Ration Heater (or FRH) is a great flavor enhancer and beloved MRE element in cold climates. Add water to the heating pouch and the heater will activate, jumping to a high temperature and staying there for about 10 minutes. Some brands, such as MREStar, use a larger amount of these heating granules, giving you enough to heat for the entrée, a side dish, and maybe even a drink. In icy emergencies, these heaters can also heat canned food and other items, or be placed between layers of clothing for a steamy body heater.

DON'T FORGET TO ACCESSORIZE Everybody needs accessories. Contemporary MRE accessory packs include a spoon, sugar packets, salt, pepper, a napkin, a wet wipe, hot sauce, and sometimes instant coffee or chewing gum. Snacks can include candy, cookies, trail mix, and beverages like milkshakes and cocoa.

STORE THEM RIGHT To protect your MREs, store them in a cool, dry environment that is rodent-free. If you cannot guarantee that rats and mice will be absent, place the MREs in a metal container.

COOL TOOLS
MREs

Most MRE pouches are retort pouches. These are tough, layered combinations of polyester, aluminum foil, and polypropylene. These pouches protect commercially sterilized food for long periods of time, unless they are pierced or handled roughly while frozen. Temperature is the biggest factor in a long MRE lifespan. Here is a breakdown of temperature and time.

TEMPERATURE	TIME IT WILL LAST
70° F (21° C)	5.5 years
80° F (27° C)	4 years
90° F (32° C)	2.5 years
100° F (38° C)	1.5 years

MREs provide high-energy menus with sugary and starchy foods

Retort pouches offer long lifespan and preserve the flavor and quality of the food inside

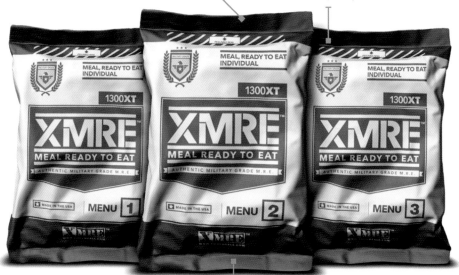

- When stored below 50° F (10° C), MREs can last for a decade or more

Most MREs contain a variety of snacks and accessories

89 SURVIVE A FALL THROUGH ICE

Even thick ice can be pocked with thin spots, which occasionally give way and drop a skater or ice fisherman into the near-freezing water. Quick action and the right tools are your best bet for surviving the icy crisis of crossing the wrong pond at the wrong time. If you're on the ice, you should have ice rescue spikes on your person; if you're skating on a pond or lake, someone should at least have a rope nearby.

If you're rescuing yourself with the picks, get to the edge of the solid ice and stab both picks into the ice. Use all your strength to haul yourself out of the hole. Then use the spikes, hand over hand, to crawl away from the hole. Once you're several yards (meters) from the hole, see if you can stand up, and make for shelter and dry clothing as fast as you can. Be alert for the signs of both hypothermia and shock.

In the event you are rescuing someone from the ice, tie a rope to a secure object and carry (or throw) the rope out to the victim. Make sure to tie a loop in the end of the rope to help him hang on. Haul him out of the hole, get him into a warm place, and monitor for hypothermia and shock.

90
DIY YOUR ICE RESCUE TOOLS

To make your own ice rescue spikes, get a hacksaw, drill, two ice picks with wooden handles (these float!), and 6 feet (2 m) of cord. Cut off half of the metal of each pick at an angle (so the pick's still pointed when you're done cutting). Drill a hole in each handle, tie the rope to each pick, and carry this with you for every trip onto the ice.

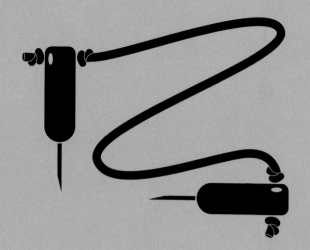

91 FOLLOW ICE DOS AND DON'TS

There's a small, nervous feeling most people have when they venture out on a floating sheet of frozen water. I'm sure our ancestors felt it, and the cautious (or lucky) ones passed it down to us. As for the people who trod upon the ice without fear or hesitation—well, let's just say that they're outnumbered by a large margin, and for good reason. Listen to that little voice of caution, and avoid ending up on thin ice—literally.

DO

Wear a personal flotation device (PFD) under your winter clothes—unless you're driving on the ice, as the excess bulk may keep you from escaping a sinking vehicle.

Carry ice rescue tools with you always. Keep them where they would be easy to reach if you end up in the water.

Have a very long length of rope that's easy to access for speedy rescues.

DON'T

Never go out on the ice by yourself.

Never forget that spring ice is NEVER safe ice.

Never test the ice by walking out without a proper plan.

92 ASSESS THE ICE

To decide if an ice-covered waterway is safe to traverse, you'll need to know the ice thickness. Using a cordless drill with a very long paddle bit and a tape measure, drill a test hole and measure it. If the ice is less than 2 inches (5 cm) thick, stay off! The weight of a person can easily break through. 4-inch (10-cm) ice (or thicker) is usually safe for walking, skating, and ice fishing on foot. 5-inch (12.5-cm) and thicker ice is probably safe for ATV or snowmobiling. 8- to 12-inch (20- to 30-cm) and thicker ice is probably safe for small cars or light pickups. Note that the words "probably" and "usually" were thrown around quite a bit. Any patch of ice can have thin spots, often due to warmer spring water or geothermal activity under the surface. And old ice, cloudy ice, and springtime ice can be unpredictable and very dangerous, despite being thick. Only go out on clear, thick ice. And above all: if in doubt, don't try it out.

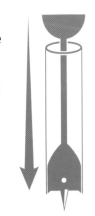

93 COME BACK FROM A COLD DROWNING

Most winters, you'll see familiar headlines in areas with treacherous ice—for example, an ice skater breaks through a frozen pond and drowns, only to be revived after a diver pulls his body to the surface. Truth is stranger than fiction: Intensely cold water can put a drowning victim in suspended animation, preventing brain damage and reducing the need for oxygen. This cold immersion slows the heartbeat, halts respiration, and redistributes blood toward the organs that need it most (the heart, lungs, and brain). The current record for near-drowning under these conditions is 40 minutes before revival, and stories of briefer submersions are plentiful. In cold-water drowning, the victim should never be considered dead until the body has been rewarmed and is still unresponsive to resuscitation.

94 PUT THE ICE TO WORK

While all due caution should be exercised—always!—when you're out on an icy body of water, it's also important to understand that the ice isn't out to get you. When used in the right way and for the right reasons, ice can become an extremely valuable resource for your survival and the survival of those around you. Here are a few ways to make the treacherous ice work for you.

BUILD WITH ICE A thin slab of ice can be used in a number of ways to help construct a survival snow shelter.

The best uses are as a nice, clear window to let in light (if you have a less cloudy and more manageable section of ice) and as a slab door (for heftier pieces). For each of these projects, select sheets of ice that are clear, free of cracks, and 1 to 2 inches (2.5 to 5 cm) thick. You'll need to be able to move them once they're in place, especially the slab door.

ASSIST YOUR TRAPS Ice slabs make excellent funnels and fencing for trap sites. Use the ice to build walls, holes, paths, gates, and other structures to help direct your prey to just the right spot. Don't worry if your structures are a bit crude—your dinner won't notice.

HEAL WITH COLD Sprains and strains are common injuries when you're in the outdoor wilderness, and relief is close at hand during the winter. Grab a chunk of ice and wrap it in cloth. Use this bundle as a cold pack to reduce swelling and pain in the affected area.

95 PREP FOR HIGH WINDS

In some areas, winter winds can be as fierce as hurricane gusts, so it's a good idea to prepare your home, business, yard, and vehicles as if a hurricane really were barreling down on you. Make these preparations and then head for cover.

- Bring in everything from the yard, like lawn furniture, toys, garbage cans, bird feeders, and other items that could become projectile missiles.

- If you have operational shutters, secure them over your windows to protect against breakage.

- Tree-proof your home in the off season (see item 99).

- Stay alert to your region's watches and advisories.

- Be ready for large snowdrifts. Depending on the wind direction, snowfall, and obstructions, you may need to dig yourself out of your home.

96 DRIVE THROUGH ICE

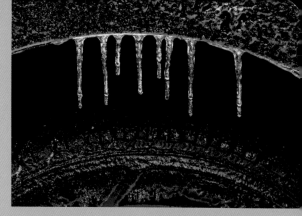

Even if you have snow tires, chains, and all-wheel drive, attempting to drive through hail, sleet, and freezing rain is downright foolhardy. Hail and sleet are created when water droplets freeze, gather more moisture, and grow too big to be supported by the air currents. Hail is more common in warmer seasons and climates, but it can occur during some winter thunderstorms—and it can fall at speeds of 100 mph (161 kph).

Since sleet doesn't form such large pellets at those heights, it falls much more slowly, but both hail and sleet can coat the roadway and turn the blacktop into a treacherous skating rink for cars. The best advice when facing a ride through ice is to rethink the plan. Your vehicle was not designed to drive on slick little balls of ice. Even a 4x4 with great tires will offer little safety. And if an ice storm is in progress, with solid sheets of ice forming on the road surface, no one is going anywhere but into a ditch.

97 TREE-PROOF YOUR HOME

Storms and heavy snow can cause the trees and branches around your home to break and fall, causing property damage and dangerous hazards. At first glance, it may not be obvious which trees need to go and which ones can stay, but follow these tips and you'll know which problem areas to point out to the pros.

STUDY THE SPECIES Some sturdy tree species are strong choices for shade and windbreaks around your home. Other species (often those that produce flowers or fruit) can be prone to breakage. Bradford pear trees are notoriously vulnerable to wind and the weight of snow and ice. Some evergreen trees are brittle as well. And certain pine species can grow to huge heights above your house and then rain down branches upon the roof.

MAKE AN INSPECTION Regardless of species, some tree traits always merit further inspection. As you regularly check for and take down dead trees around your home, you should also dispose of sickly ones, such as trees with trunk cracks or holes, or those with fungus or mushrooms growing on them (a sure sign of decay). Even the shape of a tree's forks can have a bearing on its strength. U-shaped tree forks are generally sturdy, while V-shaped forks are prone to splitting and are more likely to break and fall.

CHECK YOUR COVERAGE Most home insurance policies will cover tree-related damage, but not all policies. It pays to find out your exact coverage for damage to the structure and vehicles, as well as damage to their contents. It's far better to find out that you're not covered through a call to the company rather than through a denied claim.

98 INSPECT YOUR ABODE

After the weather finally breaks, use the window of calm to walk around your house and peer into any attics, crawlspaces, and basements to assess your home and discover any damage the winter storm may have caused. There are several elements you should check on to make sure your home successfully weathered another storm.

CHECK THE ROOF As you skirt the perimeter of your house, look for excessive snow loads, signs of ice damming, and damaged areas of the roof or chimneys. Take care of any issues you find right away.

READ YOUR FUEL GAUGES If you didn't run out of fuel during the storm, count yourself lucky. But luck has a way of running out, just like your gas tank and woodpile. After the storm clears, check on your supply of heating oil, propane, LP gas, or wood. Refill and resupply your stock as needed.

CLEAN EXTERIOR SYSTEMS Outdoor units for heating and cooling should be uncovered if they are buried beneath snow or ice. Even if you don't need the unit in the winter (like an air conditioner), it's still wise to keep it clear. A weatherproof cover would be a great investment for snowy and icy climates.

LOOK TO THE TREES Make sure the trees around your home and driveway aren't leaning in any bad directions. Trees can be incredibly heavy, and they can do a lot of damage if they hit a fence, shed, home, or vehicle. If you do spot a tree that looks like it could come down in the wrong spot, call in a pro to take it out. A professional tree crew can drop a tree right where they want it to drop (say, between your house and fence). And if they can't, a climber can cut the top out of it and drop it piece by piece until it's gone. This is one project the inexperienced should definitely not tackle on their own (see right).

CHECK FOR LEAKS Crawl through your crawlspace and amble through your attic. Look for water leaks from damaged roofing and cracked pipes caused by ice. Call in a pro if you find evidence of such damage.

99 TREAD LIGHTLY WITH TREE REMOVAL

Ice and wet snow frequently claim the weaker branches of the trees around our home, but a monster of a storm can take out massive limbs and entire trees. While you may be grateful for the free firewood, there are a few issues that can and will arise.

First of all, an overconfident yet inexperienced chainsaw operator moving around on a slick surface is just begging for trouble. Be aware that your DIY impulse can put you into harm's way when dealing with trees that have fallen on your home, leaning trees that are hung up in the top of another tree, and any trunks or limbs that are bent and under tension. Sure, it's cheaper to do the work yourself than to hire a pro, but it's also possible that you could be seriously injured or killed by falling timber. One of my father's friends was killed felling a tree many winters ago. The trunk split as he was cutting into it, and a plank under tension sprang outward. The plank hit him in the head, and that was it. Don't tempt fate. If you haven't cut down, cut up, and cut into a lot of trees, call someone who has.

100 DEFROST YOUR FROZEN PIPES

Should a cold snap freeze your pipes, it can be a tricky procedure to thaw them out again. Best case scenario: one of the water lines is slushy and can be thawed out in a few minutes. Worst case: a line has frozen and cracked, and will create a massive water leak as soon as it thaws. Here are some tips to help you through this winter plumbing nightmare.

STEP 1 Check the faucets throughout your home to see which ones are running. It may be that only one small section is frozen. If all of your fixtures stop producing water at the same time, it may be a frozen main supply line. Likely spots for freezing are pipes in exterior walls and in unheated crawlspaces.

STEP 2 Raise the temperature. If your power is restored, turn your thermostat up to allow the home to warm up. Set it to several degrees above your normal setting for the winter season. If you think the freezing occurred in a crawlspace, place an electric heater inside and monitor it closely. Leave a few faucets open so you'll know when the pipe has thawed.

STEP 3 Check for leaks. Once water is flowing to all fixtures, turn off the faucets and any noise sources in the home. Walk through the house listening intently for the sound of water spraying inside the walls, floors, or ceilings. Look in crawlspaces for rivulets of running water. If you find a leak, turn off the water and call in a professional.

STEP 4 Prevent the next freeze. Frozen pipes often occur in the same poorly heated or poorly insulated spot each winter. You can prevent further frozen pipes by adding pipe insulation or heated pipe wrap to trouble spots, and letting the water drip on particularly frigid nights. Keep in mind that it's not just the supply side—the wastewater pipes can freeze, too. If the dripping faucet has a chance of plugging up a waste line with ice, let the faucet drip into a bucket rather than into the drain.

ARE YOU READY FOR WINTER'S FURY?

The time for snowball fights and hot cocoa is over; it's now time to put your survival skills to the ultimate, deep-freeze test. In this chapter, you're out among the elements, and it comes down to just you and the cold. Whether you've gotten lost in the wintry woods or you've decided to live a life in the wilderness, the skills you'll need are the same. You have to know how to find shelter from the bitter cold, secure a water source, find food (and lots of it), stay warm, and figure out how to get from point A to point B without becoming a human popsicle. Take the lessons in this chapter to heart, because winter's not liable—nor likely—to give you a second chance.

101 SURVIVE MENTALLY

The art of survival begins not when you set up camp, but as soon as you address your mental survival game. The mental elements you need to make it through an emergency are so important, in fact, that I either begin or end most of my classes with this topic. And thanks to your ancestors, you already possess these amazing survival tools.

ATTITUDE "Positive mental attitude" can be found in every survival book, Scout manual, and wilderness class, but don't discount it as cliché or lip service—PMA is a real necessity, and may be one of the most important (and hardest) skills to master.

MENTAL TOUGHNESS I'm not talking about how much stamina or how many calluses you have. This is the strength of your will and the toughness of your mind. To be mentally tough, you must tolerate the intolerable, suffer through the insufferable, and overpower your own weakness and inclination to give up or give in.

MOTIVATION What motivates a person to stay alive, maintaining hope and endurance, when everything has gone wrong? Many survival stories involve the survivor's devotion to a higher power, or their intense desire to get back to loved ones. And a few have even credited their burning desire for revenge.

WORK ETHIC A major player in survival, your work ethic can be built up over time, just like any other skill. A survivor sticks with the job until the job gets done, and a strong work ethic can go a long way toward making up for the things that luck doesn't provide.

ADAPTABILITY The ability to adapt and the ability to survive have always been closely related. Think about plants and animals: those that cannot adapt to a changing environment die out, while the ones that adapt and change are the survivors. Learn to adapt to shifting situations, and to recognize what's worth continuing versus what needs to be abandoned for the greater good.

102 AVOID THESE PITFALLS

The human animal is a complex thing, and it's important to acknowledge the natural traits that can hinder our survival, and maybe even cost us our lives in a survival situation. Don't leave these tendencies unchecked.

PREVENT PANIC Unrestrained fear is one of your worst enemies, and it can directly lead to bad decisions, lost time, and wasted energy. Don't let fear get the better of you! Focus on small but productive tasks, and keep your imagination under control. That rustling bush won't always be a bear—just sometimes.

FIGHT PESSIMISM The opposite of PMA; a dyed-in-the-wool pessimist's fatalistic attitude can leave you feeling overwhelmed and helpless. Suck it up and try to stay as positive as you can, while maintaining a grip on the reality of the situation.

BOYCOTT LAZINESS It's hard work building survival shelters, hauling water, and carrying firewood. Survival is not a vacation. Being lazy and seeking the easiest path will eventually cause you some serious trouble. You need to honestly look at your workload, pad it a little for some extra security, and then get it done.

SAY GOODBYE TO STUBBORNNESS Stubbornness, though occasionally used for the greater good, is a refusal to adapt. It's very simple to identify, but harder to treat. Don't keep throwing lit matches into a poorly constructed fire lay; you did it wrong and you need to rebuild. Try something else, rather than blindly continuing on a path that's not working out.

ELIMINATE IGNORANCE Despite the wealth of information available today, there are a lot of people who couldn't survive their way out of a paper bag. In short, don't let other people get you killed. Many people think survival looks easy, and they vastly overestimate their ability to do anything physical. When it comes to survival skills, you need to know what to do, how to do it, and you need to have successfully practiced the skill before—and with experience comes wisdom.

103

PLAN YOUR PRIORITIES

We begin with the survival priorities. These are the tasks to accomplish and the issues to tackle, organized from the most pressing items to the lesser concerns. This is your game plan for success—don't ignore it or mix up the list on a whim. Follow these steps in order.

MAKE SHELTER Your clothing is your first line of shelter, and each layer of insulation counts. Seek shelter from the cold as best you can. You don't need tools to build small, insulated nests of natural materials or cast-off items. Think of the nests you have seen in nature, and create one that you can just barely squeeze into.

CARE FOR YOUR WOUNDS A solid first-aid kit should always be part of your survival gear.

Medical aid should be rendered after shelter is secured, unless the injury is more life-threatening than exposure. Even without a kit, you can use pressure points to slow bleeding, and treat ailments like hypothermia and dehydration.

FIND WATER Melting snow and finding a natural spring are two safe ways to get drinking water without much in the way of tools and materials. What you don't want to do is emulate the TV survival gurus who demonstrate drinking out of puddles and waterways without disinfecting the water. This is the fast track to dysentery, which can kill a healthy person when left untreated. And don't eat snow for hydration. If it's cold enough for snow, it's cold enough for hypothermia.

CREATE A FIRE Lighting a fire can be a monumental task, or even an unachievable task, in cold, wet conditions. Considering fire's myriad

uses—water boiling, heating, lighting, signaling, and cooking—you should always carry fire-building implements and backup fuel sources.

SCROUNGE A MEAL Foraging for food can be a pleasant experience that yields delicious results—when you have lots of time, leisure, and cooking tools at your disposal. But all those gourmet sensibilities go out the window when you are scavenging to stay alive. If you don't know how to identify the local wild edible plants, stick with animal foods. Most critters are safe for human consumption, as long as you cook them thoroughly to kill parasites or pathogens.

SIGNAL FOR HELP This is your golden ticket to get home. Signaling can happen after the other survival priorities have been handled, or, better still, during the procurement of your survival supplies. Signal often and in varied ways to multiply your chances of attracting help and rescue.

104 COUNT YOUR CALORIES

We've discussed the value of maintaining a survival mentality and the critical list of survival priorities. These two things are the raw material from which survival is crafted. But there is a more basic requirement that exemplifies and equates to survival: calorie count. In its basest form, survival is about mitigating calorie loss and acquiring more calories. In an emergency, you want to hold onto every calorie you can—and get more in order to sustain you going forward. Here are the two ways we can keep calories in mind during survival.

CUT YOUR LOSSES The cold can be one of the most ruthless thieves of your body's stored calories. People who become lost in a frigid landscape often suffer a fast and shocking weight loss. Even with warm bedding to sleep in and adequate clothing to wear, your body has to rewarm a lot of tissue with each breath you take. This rewarming happens through your body's efforts to ramp up your metabolism for heat, which burns a lot of calories. Consuming bad food or water is another way to lose the calorie game. If you become ill (diarrhea, vomiting, or dysentery), you lose the calories you just consumed—and sometimes more. Stop calorie losses before they occur—work a little harder to make a nice shelter, rather than wasting calories shivering each night. Make the effort to boil your water and cook your food thoroughly to prevent illness and calorie loss. Constant losses can add up to serious shortages over time.

BE CALORIE CONSCIOUS Try to find high-calorie wild foods if you're caught in a wilderness survival situation. Boost the calories you are consuming by adding a little oil to your food when you're snowed in. Survival is a balancing act of calorie gain and calorie expense. You have to bring in lots of calories and make sure your activities are worth the effort. Spending the afternoon chopping through frozen soil looking for worms doesn't quite pay for itself when worms are 1 calorie per gram.

105 CAMP IN THE SNOW

Winter camping can lead to a very enjoyable time, if you come prepared and pick a good site. Walk through these steps as you set up your temporary abode in the wintry wild.

STEP 1 Consider the safety of the site. You don't want to set up your camp in an avalanche zone, under dead trees and dead branches that may fall, or out on questionable ice. Select sites that seem hazard-free, and offer an easy escape if something goes wrong.

STEP 2 Pick a place with protection from the weather; look for hills, forests, rock outcrops, and other wind-blocking features. If you can, pick a high place where the cold air won't settle. In the northern hemisphere, south-facing hillsides catch the sun. Don't set up camp on a mountaintop, but avoid the high moisture and low temps of the valley below.

STEP 3 Select a safe fire site. Dig through snow to the bare ground, if possible, and build your fire away from overhanging evergreen boughs—otherwise that heavy snow will flop down and snuff out your fire.

STEP 4 Designate a bathroom with caution. If your campsite is remote, you'll be on your own for sanitation, so the spot should be away from camp and out of the path of travel. Digging "cat holes" in the snow will work, but make sure each "deposit" is well marked. If the ground is frozen but there's no snow, bury solid waste by covering it with debris.

106 KNOW WHEN TO BAIL

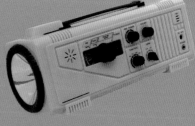

Discretion is the better part of valor—i.e. it's wise to know when to tough it out and when to bail. Just because our ancestors survived countless winters in the wild doesn't mean we have to continue on a campout gone wrong.

DON'T GET FROSTY Cold-weather injuries are no joke, and they can result in permanent damage. If you even slightly suspect frostbite or hypothermia in one of your campers, pack it up and seek professional medical care. It's all fun and snowball fights—until someone loses a few toes to frostbite or freezes to death.

STAY ALERT TO CHANGES A drastic change in the weather could spell disaster for your trip. Bring a weather radio with alert tones on winter campouts, and if worsening weather is predicted for your area, pull up stakes and head home while you still can.

107

CONSIDER THE BENEFITS

Sure, the intense cold of winter can be uncomfortable, but there are so many upsides to cold-weather camping. These are just a sampling of the many reasons to seek solace in the great—but chilly—outdoors.

BEAT THE BUGS	You might see a few bugs even in the cold, but winter camping generally lacks the relentless mosquitoes and disease-bearing ticks of bug-infested summer trips. Leave the insect repellent at home, and enjoy.
MAKE A MENU TO REMEMBER	Since food spoilage is highly unlikely, you can bring almost anything—fresh meats and sausages, cheese and butter, even ice cream and popsicles. Just watch out for freezing by keeping fresh food in a cooler without ice.
TRACK THE ELUSIVE BEASTS	Snow-covered ground exponentially increases your tracking abilities. Whether you're on a hunt or a backpacking trip, the secret stories of the animals will unfold before your eyes.
ENJOY WINTER SPORTS	Cross-country skiing, snowshoeing, ice fishing, igloo building, and many other activities are yours to enjoy during winter trips. And you might even have the place to yourself.

108

BRING THE RIGHT GEAR

The best trick for staying warm on an extended outdoor trip is bringing the right gear. Carry these items, and thank me later.

LOW-TEMP SLEEPING BAG The temperature rating on sleeping bags is generally viewed as a "survival rating" rather than the lowest temperature at which you'd be comfortable, so pick one rated to temps colder than you expect to encounter. Bags rated to -20° F (-29° C) are a common element in my camp, where the lowest temperature we'll see is 0° F (-18° C).

BOOTS AND OUTERWEAR Frostbitten digits and skin will end your fun trip in a hurry. Make certain that your clothing and footwear selections can handle the cold you'll be facing.

THICK SLEEPING PAD Nothing sucks body heat away like conduction. Lying on snow or frozen soil will be miserable and potentially dangerous, so bring a sleeping pad that is up to the task of separating you from the cold.

CAMP STOVE This little gizmo can be responsible for some of the best food and drink of your campout. For quick treats, hot chocolate, tea, and coffee can be brewed on a whim.

WINTER-WORTHY TENTS Though a tent won't exactly keep you warm, a durable tent can keep you out of the wind, snow, ice, and rain if nature decides to challenge your excursion.

109 LIGHT UP THE DARK

Plain and simple, you should be carrying multiple fire-starting methods on your person during every single outdoor excursion—especially in freezing weather. Without this precious gear, improvising a fire would be a monumental task, or, in the worst winter conditions, an impossible one. Fire equals life, and considering its many uses (boiling, heating, lighting, cooking), it makes sense to carry several faithful fire-starters.

COOL TOOLS
BUTANE LIGHTER

If I only had one survival tool, I'd probably want it to be a lighter (depending on the scenario, of course). The inexpensive and ubiquitous Bic butane lighter is a trusty source of flame, and you only need one working thumb to operate it. Which means no matter how banged-up or sore your body gets, you can create fire. One lighter has the potential to light hundreds, even thousands of fires. In addition, lighters can ignite things that methods like spark rods and magnifying lenses could never hope to successfully kindle. Keep several among your things: in your pockets, backpack, first-aid kit, and even on your key chain. The point is to have a few primary lighters at your disposal as well as several backups, so you'll never get caught without fire at the tip of your fingers.

Even if the butane runs out, the spark wheel can ignite fluffy tinder

Hold the lighter with your thumb on the edge of the red button to avoid burns from the child safety band around the spark wheel

Select a brightly-colored lighter to increase your odds of finding it if dropped or misplaced

Most lighters are waterproof and only need to be shaken or blown on to dry them out

110 TRY SOME TRICKS

Butane lighters can work fire-starting miracles, but they aren't perfect. Lighters have some quirks that need to be understood. The next time your lighter is acting up, try one of these tricks to put it back in service. You'll get a few more lights—and a few more fires—out of it.

WARM THINGS UP Temps under 15° F (-9° C) can cause the liquid butane to gel, preventing it from escaping as a gas when the button is pressed. There's an easy fix: Place the lighter inside your clothing to warm it up, and prevent the freeze-up by carrying it in an inside pocket.

SPARK A NEW FLAME If the spark wheel is damaged but there is still butane in the lighter, stick down the red button with duct tape and quickly strike sparks from a ferrocerium rod. These will ignite the gas and create the flame. Remove the tape and repeat as needed.

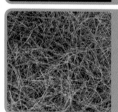

USE FLINT AND STEEL An empty lighter can still light very fine tinder. Place a tuft of cattail seed down or other plant fibers right in the mouth of the lighter. Strike the spark wheel until the fluff ignites, then quickly touch it to your tinder. This is not easy, and will take a few tries.

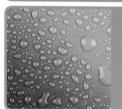

DON'T SWEAT GETTING WET Most lighters are very waterproof, so they don't need much special care (though it is smart to keep them dry if possible). If your lighter does get wet, you only need to shake it or blow on the spark wheel to dry it out and restore function.

111 10 EMERGENCY USES FOR JARS

You already know the wonders of canning jars if you are a home canner or a moonshiner: Old-timey and reusable, they're extremely versatile and have a number of survival-savvy attributes. Here are my top ten survival uses for the classic glass canning jar.

DRY FOOD PACKAGING Keep bugs, rodents, and dampness out of food stores by putting dry goods into tightly-capped jars. Add oxygen-absorber packets for best results.

TINDER BOX Keep tinder dry and away from nest-making rodents by storing a jar full of shredded bark, dryer lint, or other top-tier tinder at your camp or bug-out site.

BANK Take your valuable coins, jewelry, and other safe-worthy items, fill the jar, and bury it in a place where you'll easily find it again (but no one else will).

LANTERN Place a small candle in the jar to make a wind-proof lantern.

FIRST-AID KIT Canning jars make great, waterproof first-aid supply containers.

WILD GAME AND VEGGIE SAVER Homegrown tomatoes, caught fish, and hunted game can be stored for years if properly canned and stored in a cool, dark place.

SHARP TOOL Glass knives and arrowheads can be chipped from the pieces of a broken jar. Wear gloves and goggles and shape the pieces with a nail embedded in a stick.

HOME BREW While mixing up your own moonshine may be illegal, home-brewing wine and beer is not against the law. Store your handcrafted beverages in canning jars.

WILD PHARMACY Medicinal plants can be dried and stored for several seasons in canning jars. (The word "drug" is from the Dutch *droog*: dried medicinal plant.)

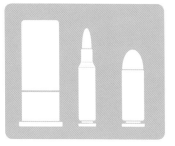

AMMO CACHE Store a few jars of your most-used ammunition by burying them at a bug-out site or in the yard. Again, make sure it's a site you'll be able to find.

112 COUNT TO TEN

Ever heard of the "Ten Essentials"? The original list of ten essential outdoor items was drawn up in the 1930s for mountain climbers and outdoor enthusiasts. A Seattle-based group called the Mountaineers designed the list for two reasons. First, it gave people a list of gear to acquire in case of emergency. Second, it provided a support system in the event that someone had to unexpectedly stay outdoors overnight (or longer). The classic ten essentials are a map, compass, sunglasses and sunscreen (counted as one item), extra clothing, flashlight, first-aid supplies, fire starter, matches, knife, and extra food. The group has since updated the list by focusing on systems rather than specific items.

The original list has some great selections in it, but jumping forward 80 years, the updated list has two game changers: Hydration and emergency shelter are the two most critical elements of survival (barring any first-aid items needed for injuries). Water and shelter are glaringly absent in the original Ten Essentials, but, thankfully for a new generation of outdoor adventurers, the updated list provides a great framework.

THE UPDATED TEN ESSENTIAL SYSTEMS

1. Navigation (map and compass)

2. Sun protection (sunglasses and sunscreen)

3. Insulation (extra clothing and outerwear)

4. Illumination (headlamp or flashlight)

5. First-aid supplies

6. Fire (waterproof matches, lighter, and candles)

7. Repair kit and tools (duct tape, multi-tool, and other tools)

8. Nutrition (extra food)

9. Hydration (extra water)

10. Emergency shelter

113

CREATE YOUR OWN KIT

Opening up a wilderness emergency kit—especially when you really need it—should feel like Christmas morning. Everything you've been dying to have (literally) is right there within your grasp. Learning from the Ten Essentials and building upon them, here's a minimum of what you should carry.

SHELTER ITEMS A space blanket, extra clothing, a bivy sack, and even large garbage bags can be handy items for shelter. Exposure is a top threat in the cold, so shelter is always your top priority.

FIRE-STARTING GEAR Another key to the cold, fire gear like lighters, waterproof matches, and other fire makers should be tucked throughout your equipment. Three ignition sources is my minimum. You should also include some fire-starting fuel, like cotton balls with Vaseline, candle nubs, or commercial fire starters.

WATER PROCUREMENT SUPPLIES A metal cup, bowl, or pot to boil water provides you with a safe and unlimited water supply. Water purification tablets and a container should also be included.

LIGHT SOURCES Bring several rugged and waterproof light sources, like a flashlight and headlamp. Don't forget to pack extra batteries.

SIGNAL GEAR Carry a whistle to signal for your buddies or for help, and a signal mirror, which can go much further. And don't forget your cell phone.

TOOLS Carry a quality knife and cordage (another vital multi-use tool). Duct tape should be part of every survival kit, and it's even flammable.

NAVIGATION GEAR You'll need a compass and local map, or a GPS with extra batteries.

MEDICAL SUPPLIES Bring a first-aid kit to treat wounds, mitigate illness, and prevent infection.

NOURISHMENT Since the cold can suck the calories right out of you, bring an emergency food supply. You'll be stronger and sleep more warmly with food in your belly. Add fishing gear and snares, which are a good backup strategy.

PROTECTION ITEMS This group is diverse and based on the hazards you'll face. Sunscreen and goggles protect your skin and vision. Bear spray fends off animals. And work gloves save your hands from the wear and tear of survival tasks.

114 BLAZE A TRAIL

Not certain you can find your way back if you head out into the wild? It can be a big problem in snowy conditions and featureless terrain. If you're short on navigational equipment but you're a crafty survivor, you can mark your own path and make it back to camp without any hassle. Use these techniques to blaze a trail across any landscape.

MAKE MARKS As you traverse forests or fields, mark your travel on prominent trees and rocks. During emergencies, high-impact marking (like chopping arrows into tree bark or chipping rock) may be a necessary method. For lower levels of distress, a simple piece of black charcoal from your campfire can be used as a pencil; draw arrows or write messages on trees, rocks, and other surfaces to mark your progress. These markings can last for months, but will eventually wear away. Always make your marks at eye level for easy recognition.

BUILD A CAIRN In rocky country, pillars of stone known as cairns are used as landmarks and waypoints. Build your own if time and energy allow, or construct a simpler version—a snowman or a cone of tall sticks. Place these in open areas to indicate the trail at a distance or to signal other information. Similarly, you can make arrows and other signs for pathfinding on the ground—but know they'll be easily buried under a light snow.

TIE FLAGS Small strips of colorful fabric or material can be used as excellent trail markers in brushy areas and woodland terrain. Plastic survey tape is my favorite to carry. Choose bright colors not found in nature, like hot pink or neon purple, for visibility. Hang small strips at eye level, within view of the last marker, and your trail will be established.

115 TRACK YOURSELF

Following your own tracks (or someone else's) falls into the fascinating realm of man tracking. This age-old art form is easy in snowy environments, and it can provide you with a viable way of getting back to camp. Follow these steps to find your own tracks and follow them back to familiar stomping grounds.

STEP 1 Move quickly! Whether you are following tracks through mounting snowfall or melting frost, move quickly for the best chance of keeping up with the disappearing trail.

STEP 2 Pay attention to your stride and gait. Depending on your height, footwear, injuries, the substrate you're walking on, and other factors, your tracks and trail should have some repeating patterns. Study the measurements of your feet, the distance and width between your footprints, and any other distinctive details.

STEP 3 Use these measurements to find any lost tracks—you'll be able to make an educated guess as to where the next set should be. You can also pick up your trail by looking for aerial signs, like broken twigs or places with knocked-down snow.

116 CARRY A COMPASS

The ancients found their way across entire seas with crude magnetic compasses, so there's no reason you can't find your way across a snowfield with basically the same tool. The modern compass allows travelers to move in a straight line even when a dark night or sudden snow squall removes all landmarks. Carry a compass and check it often, but be aware that a sensitive modern compass can react to nearby steel and other ferrous metal objects, such as gun barrels and even large belt buckles. Hold the compass away from magnetic metal objects for a true and honest reading.

117 GET LOST-PROOF

We've all been a little lost at some point, whether we were willing to admit it or not, but here's the good part—getting lost is usually one of the easiest wilderness problems to prevent. So how do we lost-proof ourselves?

- Get a map of the area that you are traveling to, and study it before going.

- Use the map and a compass (or GPS) while you are there, and always stay aware of your position on the map.

- Imagine what the terrain would look like from a bird's-eye view and visualize your place in that terrain. Think of that little "You Are Here" arrow on the big map at a trailhead, and keep it updated in your mind.

- Look behind you frequently, especially if you will be returning in that direction.

- Look for big, unusual landmarks and keep the them in view, if possible.

- Study and remember the landmarks that you use.

- When traveling off the trails, use prominent, distant landmarks and/or a compass to travel in straight lines.

- Use a "handrail." This can be a river, ridge, or any other terrain feature that gives you guidance.

And always, always, make sure someone responsible knows where you are going, and when you are coming back—just in case you get stuck somewhere.

118 CORRECT YOUR NAVIGATION

One of the trickiest elements of map and compass navigation is dealing with magnetic declination. Declination (also known as magnetic variation) is the local variance in the earth's magnetic field, and it can pull your compass needle right or left of True North—and get you properly lost.

Always take a local map with you into the wilderness, and make sure the map notes the amount to add or subtract for local declination. Magnetic declination is positive when east of true north and negative when west. Declination can make your compass reading off by as much as ten degrees, and therefore cause a person to veer way off course on long treks. Make sure you add when you should be adding, and vice versa, or your math mistake will take you even further into the wild winter.

119

BUILD A
SURVIVAL
SHELTER

In a winter wilderness emergency, shelter is going to be your top priority. If you find yourself wet or poorly dressed, hypothermia can begin to take hold within minutes, and, in harsh conditions, death can occur within a few hours. Thankfully, there are a number of survival shelter designs that can be built with few tools (or none at all) and made suitable for any landscape.

CREATE A LEAF HUT Winter isn't always about ice and snow; sometimes it's just bone-chillingly cold. In the event that there isn't any snow to fashion a shelter, build a nest out of available sticks, leaves, grasses, and other vegetation. You don't need tools—simply build a small bundle of natural materials that you can just fit inside. Make it thick and fluffy to fight against the coldest weather.

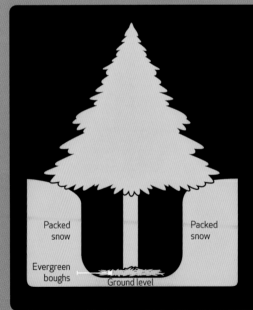

Packed snow

Packed snow

Evergreen boughs

Ground level

USE A TREE WELL In woodlands with deep snow, shelter can be as easy as a naturally occurring tree well. These are areas of lower snow density under the shelter of evergreen trees. When the snow collects on the tree boughs (rather than under the tree), it creates a natural pit which can be easily adapted into a shelter. Dig down to the bare ground, if possible, and use the snow to fill in gaps around the rim of the well. Since a fire down in this shelter would melt the snow covering the boughs overhead, your best bet for warmth is packing the cavity with insulating materials. If you can manage to find a few rocks in the snow, use a fire to warm them and place them in your bedding as heaters.

DIG A SNOW CAVE When snow
has drifted and frozen into a
solid mass, you can excavate
an excellent shelter using a
shovel, large pot, or even your
gloved hands. Add ventilation
holes and a "cold well" to give
the colder air a place to fall.
Use a backpack or block of
snow for a door, and—with
any of these shelters—pile up a
deep bed of evergreen boughs
or other insulating material.

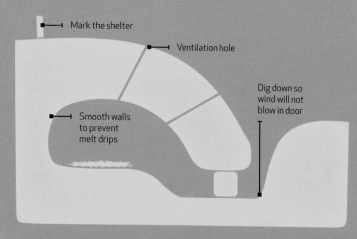

Mark the shelter

Ventilation hole

Dig down so
wind will not
blow in door

Smooth walls
to prevent
melt drips

BUILD A QUINZEE In wet,
packable snow, a quinzee
makes a great group shelter.
Pile up some gear (or snow)
and cover it with a tarp;
mound and pack more
snow on top and insert
sticks in the mound. They
should all be an equal
length of 12–18 inches
(30–45 cm). Let the pile to
harden for a few hours, then
dig a doorway, pull out the
gear (or initial snow pile),
and excavate as you would
a cave. Stop digging when
you start to hit the sticks—
this will prevent thin spots
in the dome. Add a door
and you're all set.

BUILD A SNOW TRENCH Use a saw to cut slabs out of
solid snow, creating a trench and ceiling blocks. You
can dig out a trench in softer snow, too, and cover
it with a roof of
poles, tree boughs,
and an insulating
layer of snow. This
trench is ideal for
a one- or two-
person shelter.

LAY BLOCKS FOR AN IGLOO The most impressive shelter is
the igloo, an engineering masterpiece of carved blocks
set in a spiraling dome. When properly built with the
right quality of snow, the inside can reach temperatures
above freezing from mere body heat. Start with a triangle-
shaped block, then move to trapezoidal blocks, all with
tapered edges. The final block is the keystone piece in the
center. Amateurs can build an igloo if they're good with
their hands (and
with geometry),
but the structures
will never reach
the quality of
those made by
one who regularly
practices these
skills.

120 LIGHT FIRE ON ICE

Burning a fire on top of the snow is something most people don't think about until they have to do it. In areas with little snow, you can always dig down to the soil surface to build your fire. But if the snow is deep and you lack digging tools or don't have the time, a fire on top is the best option. Less experienced outdoor enthusiasts often get a rude shock the first time they try it: The fire starts out normally enough, but then the snow beneath it melts, putting out your coals and leaving you with no fire and a jumble of wet black sticks. If you find yourself in need of a fire on top of ice, follow along and enjoy the warmth.

You'll need the material to form a raft. You can use a piece of metal—just prop some logs under it so the metal doesn't melt the snow beneath—or you can use dead wood, rotten wood, or freshly-cut (green) wood (this is always the best option). You can use whole chunks, or split your logs to create a very flat raft. Obviously, the whole pieces will last longer than split wood. Replace as needed.

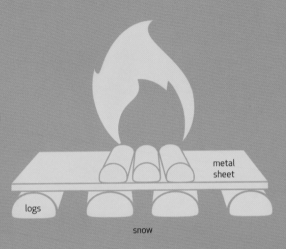

121 MAKE A SNOW SIGNAL

We've all been warned not to eat the yellow snow, but colored snow can come in handy when you need to signal for help. Depending on your resources, you may have liquids or powders with you that could be used to dye the snow and create massive ground-to-air signals. In some classic survival kits of yore, potassium permanganate was included as a water disinfecting powder—and it was also very handy for signaling, as it dyed the snow an intense purple color. Today, a bottle of green, blue, or red food coloring can be taken into snowy areas to perform the same job. Simply dilute the food coloring in water and sprinkle it across the snow. If you happen to have a spray bottle handy to dispense the liquid, that's even better. Spray or drizzle a huge X on your blank canvas, or write out a big SOS—just make sure to ration your colored dye so that you're sure to have enough to finish the job. A truncated "SO" might not get you very far if spotted from the air overhead.

122 SIGNAL FOR RESCUE

One great thing about a snowy survival scenario: Rescue signals are easy to spot against the white background. One terrible thing: A little more snow can bury your signal completely. Use these guidelines to make signals that will get noticed.

- Any rescue signal needs to be huge in order to catch the attention of aircraft. Make it high-contrast against your conveniently white background—like using dark-colored logs to build X and square shapes.

- You should be able to quickly and easily clean newly fallen snow off your signal. If those logs are dark enough, a few hours of sunlight may warm the bark enough to melt additional thin snowfalls. Think of it as a self-maintaining signal.

- A giant fire can be an excellent snow country signal. In addition to the light and smoke, the snow will melt in a circle around the fire, giving you a large, round, dark patch of ground with a fire in the center that can be seen from a low-altitude plane or search helicopter.

- Use food coloring or certain survival-kit chemicals to write your message in the snow (see item 121 at left).

- A colorful signal panel is another good way to indicate where your camp is located, especially if that panel has a contrasting color and is large enough to be seen from a distance. Don't waste your blanket—it's not big enough, and it's more valuable wrapped around you. Use a tarp or something bright or reflective, and secure it tightly.

- Don't forget to bring signaling equipment with you into the wild. Signal whistles can work day or night, even in a whiteout. Once the weather clears, signal mirrors can catch the attention of people and aircraft miles away.

123 LASH SOME SNOWSHOES

Walking through deep snow without any snowshoes is called "post holing" and it is a massive drain on your energy. Soon you'll have created what looks like a row of deep holes in the snow, and you'll be soaked with sweat and exhausted. Avoiding this situation is far easier than you'd think, if you know how to improvise some snowshoes. Take these steps toward efficient movement through the snow.

STEP 1 Collect some freshly cut sticks and some cordage material. Ten of the sticks (five for each shoe) should be the same length as the distance from your foot to your armpit. A few other sticks can be varying lengths, as they'll be cut to fit.

STEP 2 Make two bundles of five sticks and lash together one end of each bundle. Mark a point halfway down each bundle and lash on a crosspiece that is roughly 10 inches (25 cm) long. This is where the ball of your foot will pivot. Lash a similar stick about 2 inches (5 cm) in front of each of the crosspieces. This one will end up under your toes.

STEP 3 Place your foot on the shoe, with the ball of your foot on the first stick you tied. Make a mark where your heel will fall. Add another crosspiece (or two) where your heel will fall on each shoe. Lash the free ends of the long sticks together.

STEP 4 Using more cordage, tie a snowshoe to each foot. Focus on tying down the toe area of each boot, and wrap some line around your boot heel to help with snowshoe retention. Don't tie down your heel, as you'll need it to lift up when walking. Use some ski poles or improvised walking sticks to help you tread through the white stuff on your new field-built showshoes.

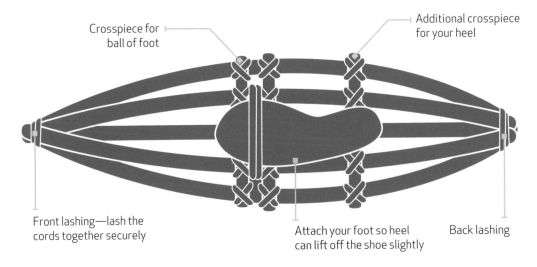

Crosspiece for ball of foot

Additional crosspiece for your heel

Front lashing—lash the cords together securely

Attach your foot so heel can lift off the shoe slightly

Back lashing

124

STUFF YOUR CLOTHES

In the event that your clothes do not offer enough insulation, you can use one of the oldest tricks in the book and stuff them like a scarecrow. The goal is to create dead air space around your body, so that the elements cannot strip away your body heat so quickly. This can be accomplished by using leaves, grass, moss, ferns, pine needles, bark fibers, and weed tops for insulation. Yes, it's a bit prickly, but do you want to be comfortable or do you want to be frozen? The stuffing can be live or dead material (dead is better), and wet or dry—but if you are already hypothermic, you'll need dry.

Ideally you'll have a loose-fitting outer layer so the stuffing isn't sitting directly against your skin—but if you only have one layer, you'll have to make do. Tuck your pants into your socks, undo your pants, fill both legs with insulation on all sides, and then try to get your pants secured again. Now tuck in your shirt, and fill the front, back, and both sleeves with insulation. A final touch is to pull on a hood or hat. You should now look like a proper scarecrow—this getup is itchy, prickly, crunchy, and ridiculous-looking, but it just might save your life.

125

PRODUCE A PROBE

Since the wind can build drifts over deep holes in the snow, hiding them from view, you should have a pole that can act as a probe in deep and uneven snowpack. The probe can also be used as a walking stick, a staff for self-defense, and even a pole for ice fishing—altogether, it's a lifesaver. Cut a sapling tree that is strong and straight, with a sturdy section that is about your height. One end can be sharpened, though it's not necessary. Use the probe by sticking it into the snow to test prospective places to step. If you feel a void or section of less resistance, don't step there! A probing tool like this can be vital when crossing glaciers and other terrain which commonly have holes, crevasses, water under the snow, and other hazardous features.

126 FORAGE FOR FOOD

The plant kingdom is a tricky place to get food in the winter, but you can pick up some calories if you are observant, lucky, and knowledgeable. Pine trees, wild syrups, and tree nuts are some of your best bets for winter plant foraging.

PASS THE PINE Pine can provide two staples: needle tea and bark flour. Use very hot water, but don't boil the needles—it'll make bitter tea and destroy the vitamin C. Don't use loblolly (eastern U.S.) or ponderosa (American southwest) pines, as these can be slightly toxic. For flour, shave off the bark's inner layer (it's rubbery and cream-colored). Dry strips until brittle and then grind them. The flour is caloric and good for blending with other flours.

BOIL DOWN WILD SYRUP Friendly and familiar, maple syrup graces many a breakfast table across the globe. But you can also use sycamore, birch, hickory, and black walnut for drinking water or for syrup. Black birch is particularly delicious. Drill a $^7/_{16}$-inch (1-cm) hole about 3 inches (7.6 cm) into the tree and hammer in a spile. Collect the sap and boil it down outdoors until you have syrup. February is the best month for sap production.

TASTE SOME TREE NUTS Tree nuts have the highest calorie density of wild plant foods. These may be a little tricky to find in the snow, but if you can identify the right trees by their bark and branch pattern, you'll know where to dig. If you're lucky and around the right species of pine trees, you may find some larger pinecones that still have nuts in them. Enjoy your snacking, straight from nature.

127

FAVOR FATTY ANIMALS

Animals have good reason to hibernate. Winter is a lean season, and for both man and beast, the colder air creates a huge drain on a body's energy reserves, making food procurement a much higher priority in a winter emergency than in a summer emergency. Adding insult to injury, food gathering is often hardest in the winter. Fortunately, there are a few high-calorie critters that won't be asleep—just less active, especially in bad weather. Don't starve to death on lean rabbit meat when there are some fattier animals that can give you the calories to survive.

NUTRITION	
BEAVER	3 ounces of beaver meat has 180 calories, half your daily iron, and many B vitamins
OPOSSUM	3 ounces of 'possum meat contains 188 calories, with lots of iron and riboflavin
CANADA GOOSE	3 ounces of skinless goose meat contains 201 calories; leave the skin on for even more
RACCOON	A 3-ounce raccoon meat serving has 217 calories, with loads of iron, thiamin, and B12

128

COLLECT SAFE WATER

In a snowy survival situation, eating the white stuff to stay hydrated is out of the question. If it's cold enough for snow, it's cold enough for hypothermia from the inside out. It would also take too long to get properly hydrated: snow is mostly frozen air (about 9 parts air to 1 part frozen water). Thankfully, snow melts, so get a fire going and fill a spare pot. You can also add another thing to your bag of tricks: the Finnish marshmallow. Don't get too excited—it's not a mallow for eating, but it bears a resemblance. It's also known as "snowman's head." To create one, select a strong, three-branched stick that resembles a trident, and skewer a large ball of snow onto the tines. Stab the base of your pole into some packed snow, or place a few pieces of firewood around the base to hold it up near the fire. Place your cup beneath and wait for it to fill up from the melting marshmallow; keep adding fresh snow to the ball to turn this into a nonstop water-dispensing machine.

129 FOIL FROZEN FIREARMS

A firearm is a game changer in many survival situations, and it's an instrumental part of a self-sufficient life in a remote area. Whether you're hunting for food or defending yourself against predators, you can't afford to have a frozen firearm at that critical moment. Use these tips to keep your weapon operational.

LUBRICATE AND WIPE Firearm lubricants are necessary to limit the wear on moving parts. Under normal conditions, natural and synthetic gun oils keep everything moving freely and help dispel the heat of the firearm's action. Few lubricants, however, can stand up to sub-freezing weather—they can become gummy or even freeze solid. To prevent this, wipe away all excess oil after lubricating your firearm components. A protective film will remain on the metal parts, but you'll remove the extra oil that could become problematic.

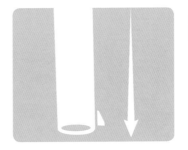

KEEP IT DOWN OUT THERE Whether a rifle is slung or handheld, a common practice among foul-weather hunters is to carry it muzzle-down. This prevents rain, ice, snow, and debris from entering the barrel.

WRAP IT UP Even with the muzzle down, parts like bolts and triggers are exposed. You can use a scabbard, though it adds weight and slows down your shooting. A silly but effective option involves ordinary plastic wrap. This clingy material is easy to remove when setting up for a shot and it conforms to the specific shape of your weapon without adding weight or bulk.

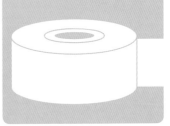

TAPE YOUR MUZZLE As an added precaution against moisture and precipitation in the barrel, place a small bit of tape over the muzzle of your weapon. Electrician's tape is a great choice. Remove it before firing, and replace after you've taken the shot.

KEEP IT COLD If you've been out in the freezing cold with your firearm and go inside for a break, leave the weapon out in the cold. If you bring it inside, condensation will form on the sub-freezing metal, and then freeze when you take it back outside, causing actions to jam, triggers to freeze, and many other dangerous problems.

130 HUNT IN THE COLD

Hunting in the cold offers some special gifts: no bugs and no spoiled meat, among others. But don't expect a wintry hunt to be a picnic; follow these steps to make your hunt safer and more productive.

STEP 1 Dress as warmly as possible—boots over two pairs of wool socks, plus extra layers of clothing. Don't forget your blaze orange.

STEP 2 Bring the right weapon and ammo to suit your target species. Some weapons are versatile, but if you try to shoot a rabbit with a big-game rifle, the rabbit that could have been your dinner will explode.

STEP 3 Set your sights, knowing that cold air is denser than warm air, so your ammunition has to push more air out of its way, stealing energy on the way to your target. If your rifle was sighted in during warmer weather, you'll need to sight it in again to compensate for the drop in the bullet due to the cold.

STEP 4 Skip the blizzard. When the weather's too nasty for the animals to be moving, you shouldn't be out there, either.

STEP 5 Many things change when hunting in the cold, so be aware of the details. Your bulkier coat may push the rifle forward, or your thick gloves could affect your feel for the trigger. If you pay attention, even the coldest climes won't keep you from your shot.

131 DIG IN

Who needs an ice axe? Ice climbers, glacier trekkers, mountaineers, and many other outdoor enthusiasts will count an ice axe (or several) among their critical gear. Think of them as giant multi-tools. They possess features for climbing, cutting, chopping, anchoring, and digging in (should you begin sliding down a sheer wall of ice or snow). There are a wide variety of ice axes on the market, some with specific functions. Straight-shafted ice axes are best for general mountaineering purposes like self-belaying and self-arrest. Curved shafts are designed for a better swing and better ice penetration, as needed during ice climbing. Whatever you're doing out there, the ice axe is a great tool.

132 CHOOSE THE RIGHT SIZE

Ice axes are measured in centimeters due to their European heritage. Common sizes range from 50 cm to 75 cm; those in the 50 cm to 60 cm range are typically used as technical ice-climbing tools, but they don't provide much leverage and are not as effective for self-arrest. Axes over 70 cm are usually too big for technical climbing—they're built for use on flatter terrain and are used for probing, glacier travel, scrambling, and creating snow anchors. When purchasing, account for your height and your likely uses. Most sporting goods and climbing gear stores will be happy to help you make your decision.

USER'S HEIGHT	ICE AXE SIZE
Less than 5'8" (<1.72 m)	50–60 cm
5'8"–6'0" (1.72–1.8 m)	60–70 cm
Taller than 6'0" (>1.8 m)	60–75 cm

133

GET CERTIFIED

The CEN (*Comité Européen de Normalisation*) is a European group that acts as a governing body for gear standards. Look for a CEN stamp on your ice axe: B-stamp axes are for general mountaineering; T-stamps are more costly, but tougher and more dependable. Some components may have different stamps, like a CEN-B shaft (light and flexible) and a CEN-T pick (for better ice penetration).

COOL TOOLS
ICE AXE

A quality ice axe has been the climbing tool of choice (aside from rope) for generations of mountaineers. These tools can be used to arrest a fall, gain ground, dig through ice and snow, and even defend yourself against a wild animal attack.

The pick is the sharp end of the ice axe, commonly used as a hook.

The adze is the chopping tool on the axe. This garden hoe–like blade is used to cut steps or seats in snow and ice.

The shaft of the axe can be carbon fiber, aluminum, or steel. The aluminum is light, but not as strong as other materials. The steel is strong but heavy. The carbon fiber is strong and light—but expensive.

The ice axe leash is for tool retention. Some axes come with pre-made leashes, or you can create a leash from either cord or webbing.

134

SPOT AN AVALANCHE ZONE

Sure, it's fun to ski off the groomed trails and trek across a snowfield, but these outdoor adventures have their hazards—especially in an avalanche area. There are many ways to avoid becoming a human popsicle: Two of the biggest factors to watch out for are recent heavy snowfall and the mountain's incline. Avalanche risks increase after a heavy snow—and the worst time of all is when warm weather or rain follows snow, and then the cold conditions return once more. The angle of the mountain slope is also a major player—most avalanches occur when the slope is 30 to 45 degrees, but even slopes of 25 or 60 degrees can slide if the conditions are right (or, from your perspective, very wrong). Here are some of the other indicators.

THE SUN'S POSITION Snow is most volatile on slopes that melt and refreeze repeatedly. During warmer winter days, plan a route that keeps you off these slopes.

YOUR EARS AND EYES Don't tread on snow that makes a hollow sound when you step on it or on any snow that looks like large, sparkly crystals instead of powder (this is deadly stuff known as depth hoar).

AVALANCHE EVIDENCE Snow debris and broken trees are signs of previous avalanches, so be especially wary of these trouble spots.

CHUTES WITHOUT LADDERS Vegetation (trees, bushes) and geological features (boulders) act as anchors for snowpack. Beware of open, chute-like areas with no trees or rocks visible. And if you're snowshoeing or cross-country skiing, stick to ridgelines, windward hillsides, dense forests, or low-angle slopes.

135 TOTE THE TOOLS

A beacon, probe, and shovel are known as the trinity of avalanche rescue. You'll need all three to rescue people quickly and efficiently, so keep these tools nearby during outings in avalanche country.

BEACON If you're crazy enough to spend time in areas with unstable snow, you'll definitely need an avalanche beacon. Turn the unit on, set it to transmit, and strap it around your waist and over a shoulder under your outer layer of clothing. Let others know your plans prior to heading out. If you end up buried in the snow, rescuers can pick up your signal and know where to start digging.

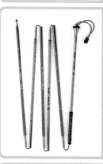

PROBE A collapsible probe is a long tool very similar to a tent pole. It's used to feel objects under the avalanche snow (like a buried person), and to focus the excavation effort. It would be impossible to dig up an entire avalanche area in a short amount of time, but a probe coupled with an avalanche beacon can allow rescuers to zero in on a victim's position.

SHOVEL A sturdy shovel is the fastest and safest way to rescue someone buried under the snow, and allows you take action pronto, should you encounter a buried victim. Every minute counts in this type of emergency, so the larger the shovel, the more time—and breath, and lives—you'll save.

136 DON'T BURY YOURSELF

Despite the "wisdom" of winter sport movies, the act of yelling or yodeling in the snowy mountains usually doesn't trigger a snow slide. But a good hard wipeout when you're skiing or snowboarding can set off a snow enthusiast–consuming avalanche, and it can even start right beneath your feet. It's true that most avalanche victims trigger the slide that buries them.

This self-activating doom is much less likely to occur on well-traveled ski slopes and trails. In addition to watching out for avalanche-prone areas, watch out for triggers from other outdoor enthusiasts—like that tumble taken by the skier up the slope from your position. And do try to keep your yelling and firecracker-lighting to a minimum.

137 BUY A BALLOON

For those who move unprotected through avalanche zones, an avalanche airbag may be the device that saves your life. These airbags are vests or backpacks with a quick-deploying balloon that allows an avalanche victim to stay above the snow, or at least higher in the snow mass. These devices are powered by air, CO_2, or nitrogen cylinders, or they are battery operated (you can usually bring the battery-powered units on commercial flights). Though they do not protect a person from the trauma of impacting rocks, ice chunks, or trees, these devices have been shown to save lives. One review found that wearing an avalanche airbag saved an average of 64 out of 100 people who would have otherwise died.

Flow of avalanche

With an airbag

Without an airbag

138 SWIM TO SURVIVE

Snow doesn't exactly move the same way water moves, but there are similarities. If an avalanche breaks loose underfoot, use these techniques to survive.

- Abandon all your equipment. Skis, poles, snowboards, snowshoes, and even snowmobiles will only get in your way, or hit you in the churning sea of snow.

- If possible, try to shelter behind rocks, trees, or vehicles. Crouch down and turn your back toward the avalanche.

- If caught in the open, "swim" through the snow and try to avoid hitting any stationary objects.

- Be aware of dangerous terrain features, like cliffs, boulder fields, groves of trees, or any other hazards.

- As the snow nears you, take a deep breath and cover your nose and mouth.

- Thrust, kick, and swim to stay on the surface. Ride on top of the snow, and attempt to get to the edge of the avalanche.

- Do not yell or open your mouth as the snow hits you, as it can fill your mouth and nose.

- As the avalanche slows, bring your hands and arms up to your face and make an air space.

139 ASSIST YOUR OWN RESCUE

Being buried under the snow is not an enviable position. But it doesn't have to be a fatal one. Once the snow stops moving, it hardens from a fluid into a cement-like consistency. Work quickly to dig your way to the surface as the slide slows. If possible, shove one arm toward the surface and move it around to create an air shaft. Use your hands to carve out a breathing space. Work methodically to avoid exhaustion. Conserve your breath by waiting

to shout until you hear rescuers above you.

If it seems possible to dig yourself out, but you're disoriented from your tumble, you'll need to know which direction is up. If the snow layer above you is relatively thin, daylight might shine through, so go towards that. If you're too deep for light to be your guide, clear a space near your mouth and spit. Watch the direction in which gravity pulls the spit, and head the other way.

140 SAVE A SNOW-BURIED VICTIM

If you are unscathed by an avalanche, but you saw someone go under, you can help him become a survivor.

- Mark the place where you last saw the victim.

- Begin looking for him directly below the last point he was seen.

- Search the greatest snow deposit first.

- Don't desert anyone trapped under the snow. They may survive for more than an hour.

- Use your phone to call for help. If you cannot call, go for help if you are certain it's only a few minutes away. Mark the route so a rescue party can follow it back.

141 SURVIVE IN AN AVALANCHE-BURIED VEHICLE

Getting buried in your vehicle may keep you alive longer than being buried without that protection, but it's still life-threatening. Take these steps to stay alive.

STEP 1 The first and most critical thing to do is turn off the engine. Running the vehicle's engine will not help you melt away your snowy covering, but it will steal your necessary oxygen. Don't smoke or burn any candles while you're buried, either. These activities will waste the precious air that you have.

STEP 2 Partially open a window to find out how deeply you are buried. Use a stick, pole, or gloved hand to see if you can find the snow's surface.

STEP 3 Use your mobile phone, radio, or any other communication device available to call for assistance.

STEP 4 Don't leave the vehicle if it doesn't seem safe to exit and stay outside. If you feel the snow may collapse on you (if you have to tunnel out) or you are in a remote area with no shelter available, try to create a ventilation tunnel and stay in the car for shelter.

142 KNOW YOUR FOE

Most animals aren't going out of their way to get you. They're just trying to stay alive like the rest of us. But when a desperate animal and an unlucky human cross paths, nature tends to take its course. To prepare for these run-ins, learn the habits and behaviors of the dangerous animals you may face.

MOUNTAIN LIONS Also known as cougars and pumas, mountain lions grow larger in areas closer to the polar regions. They are ambush predators who favor attacking from high vantage points, and they love fast-moving prey. Stay wary around rock outcrops where they could be lurking, and if you end up staring one down, raise your arms to look bigger, then yell at the animal to see if it retreats. If it doesn't, be ready to fight it off.

WOLVES The gray wolf is the largest wild canine of the Northern Hemisphere. Also known as the timber wolf and western wolf, it favors remote wilderness areas. Wolf attacks are very rare outside of Europe and Asia—but wolves can carry rabies, which changes their behavior. If you're attacked, climb the closest tree, and be prepared to live up there until they move on or rescue arrives. Hope you brought a phone with good signal up there.

POLAR BEARS Carnivorous polar bears primarily live within the Arctic Circle. They are sneaky hunters, often described as appearing from nowhere. While brown bears often maul people and leave them alive, polar bears typically kill and eat their human prey (when hungry enough)—so quick escape (in a vehicle) or defense with a firearm (killing the bear) are necessary when dealing with a polar bear that is interested in human activity.

143 PUNCH A POLAR BEAR

In July of 2010, 67-year-old Wes Werbowy had a very unusual encounter with a polar bear, and he prevented the animal's attack by punching the bear in the face—a last-ditch survival technique he learned from an Inuit elder.

Werbowy, a longtime wilderness consultant, was camping near Whale Cove, Nunavut, where he was training three Inuit hunters to be eco-tour guides. The four men had set up a camp, with separate sleeping and cooking tents to minimize the chances of a bear attack while they slept. Apparently, that wasn't effective, because just after 3 a.m. Werbowy awoke to the sound of a polar bear snuffling around outside his tent. The front of his tent collapsed as the bear pushed his head inside—the bear was less than a meter from Werbowy's face and standing on his gun. It's then that Werbowy recalled something that an Inuit elder once told him to do: punch a polar bear in the nose. Believing this might be his end, he held nothing back and slugged the massive white beast in its tender black nose. "I quite believed it was going to be the last thing I ever did, so I might as well do a good job," he said. The bear withdrew and disappeared. When the story went public, local elders praised Werbowy's bravery and wanted to shake the hand that punched a polar bear. The elders also believed that Werbowy performed a great service to the community, as that bear would not be likely to approach humans again.

Obviously, a little prevention is a safer strategy than waiting to see if a solid sock in the nose will work. It's always best to travel in groups in polar bear country. Stay alert to your surroundings and set up a tripwire perimeter around your camp at night. Steer clear of female bears with cubs, as they may attack in defense of their young. And keep food out of the equation by storing all food and garbage in bear-proof containers outside your camp area. Finally, stay away from seals, as these are the polar bear's primary food source.

144 PACK SOME BEAR SPRAY

Contrary to the name, bear spray isn't just for bears. It can be used on all kinds of two-legged and four-legged threats. Certainly a great item for bear country, it's also a safety net for any other landscape in which you're not at the top of the food chain. Get the best bear spray that money can buy by ensuring that it's EPA registered, sprays over 25 feet (8 m), and has an orange colorant. Color is a deterrent to intelligent creatures such as bruins, who are instinctively afraid of new things. They are not accustomed to an orange stinging cloud in their face, so they'll run off, then look back, trying to figure out what just happened. Meanwhile, you should be moving the other way. When used against a smaller predator, employ the same technique: Spray him in the face and get away while he's disoriented. A good policy with any threatening beast is to unload only half the canister. Save some spray for a backup shot.

145 10 EMERGENCY USES FOR BANDAGES

There's a good chance that if you have a first-aid kit, there's at least one triangle bandage in there. And while it's mostly used as a sling, this isn't the only purpose it can serve. Here are ten other ways you can use a triangle bandage in a survival or medical emergency.

WATER FILTER Though the cloth won't screen out any pathogens, pouring water through the cotton bandage will clean up the water and remove some of the sediment.

FIRE! This one's the flashy and destructive option. Triangle bandages are often cotton, which burns quite well—and it will burn even better if you add a little oil.

36" x 36" x 51"
(91cm x 91cm x 130cm)

Triangular
Bandages
Polybagged
Latex Free

dynarex

Manufactured for:
Dynarex Corporation
Orangeburg, NY 10962
www.dynarex.com

Made in China

Reorder No

BREATHING MASK In dusty or smoky situations, the bandage can provide a rudimentary dust and particle mask. Dampening the cloth works even better.

CORDAGE Tie up more than just an injured arm. The bandage can be twisted to use as a short, fat cord, or cut into strips and twisted for string.

WARMTH Tie it around your neck for a gaiter, tie it around your ears for earmuffs, or tie it around your face as a mask to stave off frostbite.

HAT Keeping your head covered will help keep you warm. Use the bandage as an improvised head covering.

CONTAINER Tie the opposing corners of the dressing together to make a bag. Or fold the triangle bandage and sew it to create a pouch.

COLD COMPRESS To treat fevers, sprains, and even venomous bites, wet the cloth bandage or fold it with snow or ice inside for a cold compress.

EYE PROTECTION Depending on the weave, you may be able to tie a strip over your eyes to protect them from sun and dust, ice, or debris.

TOURNIQUET Tie the bandage around the wounded extremity, slide a strong stick underneath, and twist. Use only for severe and unstoppable blood loss.

146 DISCOVER DOG SLEDDING

History is full of remarkable stories about the relationship between mushers and their dogs, and dog sledding has saved lives by providing rapid transportation in otherwise impossible conditions. Delivering medicine, messages, and the wounded, dog sledding has inspired literature and become an iconic part of northern culture. Mushing is far more than a sport or a pastime—in places with long, cold winters, it is a way of life.

You've seen the movies: someone yells "Mush!" and a team of dogs starts to run. But not all sled dogs are trained to respond to that word (which is probably a corruption of the French word *marche*—to go, run, or march). Although team drivers are still called mushers and "mush" is used in some training, it's soft and indistinct—sharp, distinctive commands are truly best. If you ever end up behind a team of trained dogs, learn the lingo.

COMMON COMMANDS

HIKE	All dogs should get moving (*mush* and *all right* are also used)
GEE	Turn to the right
HAW	Turn to the left (*gee* and *haw* are also used with pack animals)
EASY	Team should slow down
KISSING SOUND	Team should speed up
ON BY	Team to pass by another team or a distraction without stopping
WOAH	Stop! This is hardest for a young dog (and natural runner) to obey.

147 EAT A WINTER FEAST

Due to the short, chilly summer and long, deep winter, it's not possible to grow food crops in the Arctic. But the Inuit have always been hunters and anglers, relying heavily on high-calorie animal foods to survive.

In an ancestral diet, as much as 75% of the daily energy intake comes from fat (seems counterintuitive for a healthy diet, but you can't argue with the facts). Here's a traditional menu from a place that's too cold to farm.

FISH Fish play a big role in ancient and modern diets.

ARCTIC BIRDS Numerous species provide meat, eggs, and feathers for projects.

ARCTIC HARE AND FOX Both of these rivals have ended up in many an Arctic stew pot.

SEAL Seals are hunted for their meat and fur, and the liver has a higher level of vitamin C than many other animal foods.

POLAR BEAR Hunted for food and as predator control, the polar bear's liver can be dangerously high in vitamin A.

WILD PLANTS Harvested in summer and dried for winter, the Arctic's edible tubers, roots, berries, and seaweed give needed variety to the menu.

WALRUS Less desirable than seal (and more dangerous), walruses are still eaten today. Go easy on the liver, as its high vitamin A levels can be fatal.

WHALE Beluga and bowhead whales are still hunted for food; one juvenile whale can feed a community for many months.

CARIBOU AND MUSK OX Large animals are valuable for their meat, fat, organs, and hide.

148 WIELD A LEISTER

A traditional arctic fish spear, sometimes called a leister, is one of the most effective fish spears ever designed. The angled opening acts as a funnel to align the fish into the center of the spearhead, and one thrust impales the fish with three points. This allows the spear's user a greater margin of error, and it helps to account for the fish's movement and the deceptive refraction of the water. Whether you're fishing in the Arctic or the tropics, the traditional wisdom poured into this spear's design will give you the best chance of putting fish in your belly.

STEP 1 Select a sturdy pole to act as your spear shaft. It should be thicker than your thumb and as long as you are tall. Also collect wood, bone, antler, or metal pieces to create the spear's fork and barbs.

STEP 2 Carve and sharpen the center prong for the spear. Drill a hole in the end of your spear shaft to fit, and glue it in place.

STEP 3 Drill and insert the barbs for both sides of the spear fork. Glue and tie the fork pieces in place at the spear's end.

STEP 4 Use the spear by stalking carefully to the water's edge and holding the spear's tip near the surface. When a promising target is spotted, aim below the fish (to allow for the refraction of the water) and thrust. With any luck, you'll have fish for dinner.

149 HIKE A GLACIER

Glaciers are bodies of slow-moving ice that constantly creep downhill under their own weight. Found on every continent except Australia, they are treacherous to cross and best approached cautiously as a group. Take these steps to pick the safest path.

STEP 1 Consider crossing only if you are with a group of people and can be roped together for safety. If one person falls into a snow-covered crevasse, the others can pull him up.

STEP 2 Plan your route. If you can get to a vantage point that allows you to look down upon the glacier, use that opportunity to select several paths across the ice. Pick what appears to be the safest route, but keep the other routes in mind as backups. Use binoculars to look for solid ice and to spot any features that should be avoided.

STEP 3 Scout the dangers. The lead person should move slowly and carefully across the glacier, using a pole or long-handled ice axe to test their upcoming steps. Snow and ice can frequently cover holes and crevasses. This lead person should be roped into a harness attached to the followers; if possible, only step where your scout stepped.

150 BECOME A CAVE DWELLER

The lure of exploring natural cave shelters is almost inescapable. But before you decide to trade your campsite for the cave lifestyle, it's important to understand the hazards and best practices.

BE CAREFUL WITH FIRE Not only is the smoke harmful to cave ecosystems (I know, not a chief issue in a survival event), the heat can cause the rocks overhead to collapse (now I've got your attention). It's never safe to burn a fire inside a cave—plus, it's smoky and miserable. Make your fire outside of the cave mouth to keep out most of the smoke while radiating heat inside.

MEET THE NEIGHBORS You may not run into a Yeti, but there are plenty of other creatures to contend with. In warmer areas, snakes and bats hibernate in caves, and in colder climates, you may find predators who don't take winter naps. Be alert as you inspect, and don't expect to be alone.

SHELTER WITHIN A SHELTER Our forebears were no dummies. Plenty of evidence illustrates that our ancestors used tents or other shelters within their caves. If your stony lair is big enough and you have a tent to pitch, take advantage of the same double-shelter concept. Since caves are cold and drafty by nature, it's only sensible to add another layer of protection and warmth.

MOVE YOUR FOOD The scent of food can be a powerful lure. I once lured a beast into my cave campsite with only the aroma of dirty dishes. Thankfully, it wasn't a bear or a cougar—just a skunk. But I'd still rather not be backed in with no exit. Store all food and items with interesting odors (soaps and toothpaste) outside—use a bear vault or a bear bag.

151 LEARN TO TIE A PRUSIK

The Prusik knot (named after Austrian mountaineer Karl Prusik) is an adjustable slide and grip knot, often used as a loop on another rope. Use the Prusik to create a sling attached to climbing ropes for glacier travel—it can be used for self-rescue after a fall, and as an anchor.

To tie it, you need a short rope and a long rope. Tie a loop in the short rope and secure with a solid knot. Wrap the loop around the long rope three times, with each wrap lying flat. Pass the loop of short rope under itself and pull it tight. As long as there is some weight on the loop, the Prusik will grip the long rope.

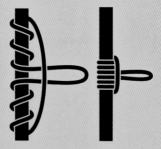

152 MAKE A HOLE FOR FISHING

Whether for sport or emergency calories, ice fishing can provide much-needed nutrition when the rest of the environment is a frozen wasteland. Ice fishing is full of traditions and a few hazards, but when done correctly (and with luck), it rewards the angler handsomely. But before you can catch anything, you need to open a hole in the ice.

BE TRADITIONAL Our ancestors dug holes with hand tools, and it still works. Heavy, sharply pointed, long-handled ice chisels (sometimes called spuds) are a common way to chop a hole through the ice. Other tools include hand-turned augers to drill, and skimmers to clear ice chunks and slush from the hole.

GO FOR POWER A more modern and speedy approach is the use of a motor-driven auger. One person can operate smaller units, while larger drills really require two people to be safe. If you ice fish frequently, it could be a worthwhile investment. You could also try your luck using a chainsaw to cut a block out of the ice, though it will need to be chopped up to be removed from the hole. Use vegetable oil for chainsaw bar lube around the ice, since motor oil and typical chainsaw lubricants are fairly toxic to aquatic life.

TRY A PRIMITIVE APPROACH If you lack both tools and technology, step back in time a few thousand years and use something your ancestor would have used: a hot rock. Burn a large fire on the shore, and heat up a large stone. Make sure you collect the rock from a dry location, as waterlogged stones tend to explode. After an hour of heating the rock in the fire, use a shovel (ideally long-handled) to carry the dangerously hot stone to your ice fishing spot. It will begin to melt the ice immediately and work its way downward— and soon your ice fishing hole will be open, smooth, and ready to fish.

153

BRING THE RIGHT TACKLE

The wrong bait or the wrong fishing technique can leave you out on the ice with no reward. Before you risk your safety, make sure you are bringing the right tools, tackle, and companions to be successful.

YOU'LL NEED

- ☐ Tools to safely open the ice, and a buddy who can help if you fall through—or a rope tied to a tree

- ☐ Bait, hooks, and line that can handle the largest local fish

- ☐ Weights to drag your line to the bottom (a common hangout for cold water fish)

- ☐ Brightly colored lures, to attract fish in the dark water

- ☐ Jigging rods, which are very simple short fishing poles that make it easier to jiggle lures and bait

- ☐ Bait backups for finicky fish—spoon lures, bait flavorings, salmon eggs, maggots, or worms

- ☐ Tip-ups: devices that hold the line for you and indicate when a fish has tugged at the bait

154

FISH ON THIN ICE

Taking the hot rock ice-melting technique a step further (see item 152), you can also go ice fishing when the ice is too thin to support your weight. This technique allows you to fish in winter waters that would normally be out of reach.

STEP 1 NEVER step out on thin ice! If you're not sure where the ground and ice meet, dig down through any snow cover to find the border.

STEP 2 Heat up a medium-sized stone, roughly the size of a melon, in a hot fire. If necessary, use the wooden raft technique (see item 120) to burn a fire on top of the snow. Heat the stone for about one hour. While the stone is heating, find a 1-yard (1-m) stick with a stout fork at the end.

STEP 3 Once the stone is hot, use the forked stick to roll the hot rock from the fire to the edge of the ice. When ready, give the stone a hard shove with the forked end of the stick to slide the rock out onto the ice. Just like shuffleboard!

STEP 4 When the stone stops sliding, it will begin to melt a hole, and should completely drop through the ice within a minute or two. Now you can cast your fishing line past the hole and drag it over the opening until it drops in the hole. Once a fish has taken the bait, gently haul it out while remaining safely on shore.

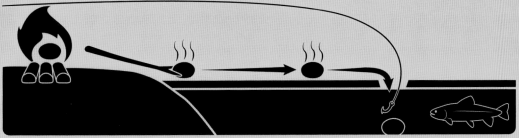

155 SNOWMOBILE SAFELY

In the depths of winter, places with ample snowfall can see their fair share of snowmobiles—either as recreation or transport. They're obviously great in cold wilderness situations, but make sure to take some precautions before your first ride of the season.

LEARN THE LAW Find out your local laws. Most areas require registration and insurance for all machines.

MAKE YOUR INSPECTION Check the oil (in four-stroke engines) and gas before you even start the engine. Make sure it's all running properly—and make sure you're stocked with emergency supplies, too.

SKIP THE BEER Don't drink and drive any vehicle. Risks skyrocket—and it's illegal.

TAKE A LESSON If you're a beginner (or just a bit rusty), consider taking a lesson or two. It's more like operating a motorcycle than a car, and it's not as easy as it looks.

DRESS FOR THE WIND Even in still weather, riding a snowmobile simulates a strong breeze and can lead to frostbite in a hurry. Wear the right clothing and keep all skin covered when the temperatures are below freezing.

TELL SOMEONE Always tell another person your destination before you leave, in case you don't come back as planned.

156 MAKE EASY REPAIRS

Snowmobiles are powerful machines, but they are vulnerable to breakdowns. Learning to make these field repairs can keep your machine purring like a kitten—a snow-devouring, smoke-spitting kitten.

REVIVE A BATTERY One common problem is the small battery losing its charge in the cold. Use standard jumper cables and another machine.

FREE A FLOODED ENGINE An engine flooded with gasoline (not water!) is a fairly easy thing to handle: Just give it some time. If there's fuel in the tank and the lines, and the fuel pump feels like it's running (feel for vibration), your engine may not start because it's flooded. Let it sit for several minutes and try it again—just once. Don't keep flooding it. Let it sit longer if a second try is needed.

OPEN AN AIRLOCK If you're stopped because you ran your gas tank dry, it may not be as simple as adding fuel, as air can fill the fuel line and prevent the new fuel from reaching the engine. If you suspect this, disconnect the fuel line nearest to the engine and turn the ignition key. This should pump fuel through the line and expel the air.

157 CARRY BACKUP GEAR

Storage space is limited on many snowmobiles, but that's no excuse to ride off without backup gear. Invest in a cargo rack, or bring a backpack with supplies. Start with this list, and build up your safety net based on how far you're going.

TOOLS You may be able to field-repair some of the common snowmobile issues. Bring a hammer, adjustable wrenches, pliers, duct tape, screwdrivers, and a multi-tool—at a minimum.

FIRE STARTERS Matches, lighters, spark rods, tinder, candles, fire-starter products—bring them all. A fire could keep you alive and ward off dangerous animals if your machine breaks down in a remote area.

WATER Safe drinking water is a vital item in any vehicle and in any climate. Use containers that won't burst when they freeze. Stick a frozen bottle inside your coat to thaw it without fire.

JUMPER CABLES Batteries can easily go dead in the deep cold. Make sure at least one person in your group has a small set of jumper cables.

FLASHLIGHTS You know the dark is coming. Keep several lights and spare batteries.

SHELTER A space blanket, emergency bivy, or some other kind of small shelter item should be included with your emergency gear in case you are stranded overnight.

FOOD In line with bringing shelter items, bring some food in case your expedition runs longer than expected due to an emergency.

WHETHER WINTER HAS JUST SETTLED

around you or you've been in its grip for months, there

is a truth that offers comfort: Winter doesn't last forever.

You've planned and prepared, and the warm return

of the sun will be your reward for surviving another

snow. But even with an end in sight, don't lose focus.

Winter weather can be as severe as it is unpredictable.

Whether it's a late-season storm or a sudden frost on

your budding garden, winter can always come up with

one last laugh. So use the skills in this book to prepare

yourself for the season, deal with emergencies, and

conquer the cold, hard bite of winter weather.

Best wishes and stay safe,

Tim MacWelch

INDEX

INDEX

CREDITS

All **PHOTOS** by Shutterstock except: 13: Adam Levy; 45:
Andrew Hetherington; 51: Point Six Socks; 79: Rocky S2V;
85: Heat Max; 88 (Cool Tools): XMRE Meals; 133: DMM
Climbing; 135 (Beacon): PIEPS; 135 (Probe) Arva Corp; 135
(Shovel) Mountain Safety Research.

All **ILLUSTRATIONS** by Conor Buckeley.

ABOUT THE AUTHOR

Tim MacWelch is the author of the *Prepare for Anything Survival Manual* and the *Hunting & Gathering Survival Manual*, and has been an active practitioner of survival and outdoor skills for over 27 years. His love of the outdoors began at a young age, growing up on a farm in Virginia, where eating wild berries, fishing, and learning about the animals of the forest were all part of country life. Tim became interested in survival skills and woodcraft as an offshoot of backpacking as a teen—while out in remote areas, it seemed like a smart plan to learn some skills. The majority of his training over the years has involved testing survival skills and devising new ones, but the biggest leaps forward came from his experience as a teacher.

Tim's teaching experiences over the years have been rich and diverse, from spending hundreds of hours volunteering to founding his year-round survival school 19 years ago. He has worked with Boy Scouts, youth groups, summer camps, and adults in all walks of life, as well as providing outdoor skills training for numerous personnel in law enforcement, search and rescue organizations, all branches of the United States Armed Forces, the State Department, and the Department of Justice and some of its agencies. Tim and his school have been featured on *Good Morning America*, several *National Geographic* programs, and in many publications including *Conde Nast Traveler*, the *Washington Post*, and *American Survival Guide*. Tim has written hundreds of pieces for *Outdoor Life* and many other publications. You can read past articles and galleries at outdoorlife.com and learn about the survival school at www.advancedsurvivaltraining.com.

ABOUT THE MAGAZINE

Since it was founded in 1898, *Outdoor Life* magazine has provided survival tips, wilderness skills, gear reports, and other essential information for hands-on outdoor enthusiasts. Each issue delivers the best advice in sportsmanship as well as thrilling true-life tales, detailed gear reviews, insider hunting, shooting, and fishing hints, and much more to nearly 1 million readers. Its survival-themed Web site also covers disaster preparedness and the skills you need to thrive anywhere from the backcountry to the urban jungles.

ACKNOWLEDGMENTS

Where would I be without *Outdoor Life* magazine and Weldon Owen publishing? Dead in a ditch somewhere outside Tijuana? No, probably nothing that dramatic, but I definitely wouldn't have four published survival books with my name on the cover. I want to thank John Taranto, Andrew McKean, and all of the other wonderful folks at *Outdoor Life* for their tireless work and endless support. I'd also like to sing the praises of my editors at Weldon Owen, Mariah Bear and Bridget Fitzgerald. They could edit a book about a fried egg and make it funny, compelling, sad, grammatically correct, and a bestseller. And I can't send enough thanks to our artists and designers at Weldon Owen, and our sales folks at Bonnier. You've made my books look amazing and you've shared them with the world. Finally, I'd like to thank my family for their patience and support while I became a recluse to write this book. Thanks and God bless you all.

weldon**owen**

President & Publisher Roger Shaw
Associate Publisher Mariah Bear
SVP, Sales & Marketing Amy Kaneko
Finance Director Philip Paulick
Editor Bridget Fitzgerald
Creative Director Kelly Booth
Art Director William Mack
Designer Allister Fein
Illustration Coordinator
Conor Buckley
Production Director Chris Hemesath
Production Manager
Michelle Duggan
Director of Enterprise Systems
Shawn Macey
Imaging Manager Don Hill

Weldon Owen would like to thank
Katharine Moore and Kevin Broccoli
for their editing and indexing services.

© 2015 Weldon Owen Inc.
1045 Sansome Street, suite 100
San Francisco, CA 94111
www.weldonowen.com

BONNIER

ISBN 978-1-61628-969-0
10 9 8 7 6 5 4 3 2 1
2015 2016 2017 2018
Printed in China by RR Donnelley

OUTDOOR LIFE

Vice President, Publishing Director
Gregory D. Gatto
Editorial Director Anthony Licata
Editor-in-Chief Andrew McKean
Executive Editor John Taranto
Managing Editor Jean McKenna
Senior Deputy Editor John B. Snow
Deputy Editor Gerry Bethge
Assistant Managing Editor
Margaret M. Nussey
Assistant Editor Natalie Krebs
Senior Administrative Assistant
Maribel Martin
Design Director Sean Johnston
Art Director Brian Struble

Associate Art Directors
Russ Smith, James A. Walsh
Photography Director John Toolan
Photo Editor Justin Appenzeller
Production Manager Judith Weber
Digital Director Nate Matthews
Online Content Editor Alex Robinson